POLICY AND PRACTICE IN EDUCATION
NUMBER EIGHTEEN

BETTER LEARNING, BETTER BEHAVIOUR

POLICY AND PRACTICE IN EDUCATION

POLICY AND PRACTICE IN EDUCATION

SERIES EDITORS
JIM O'BRIEN and CHRISTINE FORDE

BETTER LEARNING, BETTER BEHAVIOUR

George Head

Senior Lecturer,
Department of Educational Studies,
University of Glasgow

DUNEDIN ACADEMIC PRESS
EDINBURGH

Published by
Dunedin Academic Press Ltd
Hudson House
8 Albany Street
Edinburgh EH1 3QB
Scotland

ISBN 978-1-903765-67-8
ISSN 1479-6910

British Library Cataloguing in Publication data
A catalogue record for this book is available from the British Library

Typeset by Makar Publishing Production
Printed in Great Britain by Cromwell Press

CONTENTS

SERIES EDITORS' INTRODUCTION

This volume focuses on those children and young people who are regarded as 'different' because their behaviour has been perceived as difficult by society and by schools and teachers. In a period when inclusion policies are paramount, young people experiencing social, emotional and behavioural difficulties (SEBD) continue to be marginalised and present challenges to educational policy-makers, school managers and teachers.

Dr Head outlines the historical background to the issues associated with behaviour and learning and associated support before considering the issues that confront us today. He indicates that there have always been young people whose behaviour has been regarded as problematic by adults and who pose a series of challenges for society but the critical issue is how society and schooling relate to such behaviour. This tracing of the development of policy and practice proffers a critique of the *charitable* model and its associated deficit concepts such as beneficence, containment and remediation; the *needs* model and Warnock's continuum of special needs and resultant optimism about progress; and the more recent *rights* model adopted with its emphasis on inclusion.

He goes on to assess the impact of dominant theories of behaviour and provides a critical analysis of legislation, policy and practice, informed by consideration of the series of national reports and codes of practice which have emerged in the past few decades. The author suggests that the various approaches and interventions retain elements of deficit and disability. Brief case studies are used to illustrate arguments and recent Scottish research is considered to highlight innovative approaches, identify possible contradictions and to determine the current state of teacher perceptions of SEBD and school practice. Another key issue explored is what professional development might prove beneficial to enhancing the 'affective curriculum' and creating a context of inclusion where provision for young people experiencing SEBD requires a refocusing on their learning with the resultant *Better Learning, Better Behaviour*.

Dr Jim O'Brien
Vice Dean and Director,
Centre for Educational Leadership,
Moray House School of Education,
The University of Edinburgh

Dr Christine Forde
Senior Lecturer in Educational Studies
The University of Glasgow

ACKNOWLEDGEMENTS

This book draws on a number of jointly authored previous publications. My co-authors on these publications are Billy O'Neill, a former teaching colleague, Jean Kane and Nicola Cogan of the University of Glasgow and Sandy Jamieson of East Renfrewshire Council. I would like to thank all of these people for the part they have played in developing my thinking concerning the learning of young people who may be experiencing social, emotional and behavioural difficulties. I would also like to thank them for the contributions that our collaboration has made to this book. In addition, I would like to thank those colleagues from the Faculty of Education at the University of Glasgow who have read and commented on chapters for me and who have given their valuable time to discuss and help me clarify my ideas and arguments. Any inaccuracies or infelicities are entirely mine.

Finally, I would like to thank Flora and Alasdair for their patience and support.

Chapter 1

PROVISION AND PRACTICE

Young people experiencing social emotional and behavioural difficulties have been patronised, demonised and marginalised. This has been the case within Scottish society generally where they have been described either as 'vulnerable' or in pejorative terms such as 'neds' and 'yobs', depending on the circumstances. As a consequence of a disparity between a desire to support young people and how that support has manifested itself in reality, it has also been the educational experience of a group of children and young people with whose behaviour schools have found it difficult to cope, that they have been described in similar terms of personal deficit and that their learning has been consistently marginalised. This is a strong claim and requires detailed explication, which is the purpose of this chapter and, indeed, the remainder of the book. On the surface, the opening statement can be interpreted as a criticism of the Scottish education system, schools and teachers, and one that favours a particular group of young people. However, schools do not exist in a vacuum and the structures, relationships and philosophies that dominate the experience of school reflect the structures that are dominant in society in general. The purpose of this book, therefore, is to explore the relationships among schools, educators, government and, where appropriate, wider society and how these relationships impact on the educational provision and practice for children and young people who may be experiencing social, emotional or behavioural difficulties (SEBD).

An example of the nature of this relationship as it is played out in Scottish society (and hence schools) can be found in the recent document *Better Behaviour – Better Learning* (SEED, 2001). The title, and hence the approach adopted in the content, of the document is significant. The word order indicates an assumption (explored in greater detail in Chapter 3) that if teachers deal with difficult pupil behaviour as a first step, then the young people will learn better. This argument reflects the thinking in wider Scottish society that some young people's behaviour is socially unacceptable and needs to be 'fixed' (usually through punishment) if they are to become accepted members of the community. Decisions regarding the degree to which a young person's behaviour is unacceptable, where, how and by whom it will be 'fixed', are taken by adults, including professionals from law, social work and education, often with little or no consultation with the young person (the children's hearing system being a notable exception). The hierarchical, patronymic structures that dominate wider society are reflected in schools and, therefore, it is not surprising that similar thinking dominates approaches to the learning of young people.

The document, therefore, can be seen as patronising in that it assumes that the 'solution' to indiscipline in schools lies in what head teachers and teachers choose to do to and for pupils. School managers and teachers are assumed to be in a privileged position of power in relation to their pupils but the structures which serve to confer power on them are neither questioned nor challenged. Secondly, the document can be seen as demonising in that, whilst wishing to improve the context of the learning of young people who may be identified as troublesome, it is nevertheless posited on an assumption of deficient behaviour on the part of young people. In addition, whilst recognising the spurious nature of indiscipline and behavioural difficulties, it offers little in the way of practical approaches but rather assumes that schools and teachers will somehow be able to identify individuals who fit into the category and will treat them in appropriate ways. Finally, the document is marginalising in that, whilst it recognises behavioural difficulties as a learning difficulty that should be addressed in the same way as any other learning difficulty, it nevertheless argues that measures be taken to 'fix' the behaviour and assumes that, thereafter, learning will take place. This is in direct contrast to the learning of all other young people, including those with other learning difficulties, in that schools and teachers are not expected to 'sort' the difficulty (for example, visual impairment or hearing impairment) before they deal with the pupil's learning.

In the following part of this chapter, the reactions of UK society generally to children and young people who have been perceived as being different because their behaviour has been difficult is traced in order to develop an understanding of the thinking behind the document. In the context of the twenty-first century, it becomes necessary to explore approaches to the learning of young people whose behaviour schools find difficult in a context of inclusion. Finally, an analysis of the historical context that challenges traditional identities of pupils and teachers in the interface that is the learning of young people who might be experiencing social, emotional and behavioural difficulties is offered. This structure presents a route into understanding why educational provision for this group of children and young people takes its current form.

A historical context

There have always been children and young people whose behaviour has disturbed or perplexed adults. In Classical times, matters that could not be understood otherwise were sometimes explained by mythology. Classical mythology abounds with tales of young men and women whose adventures could be described as foolish in the extreme or detrimental to the well-being of others. Two examples of behaviour from Classical mythology can be used to illustrate parallels with some of the behaviours that might be exhibited by some young people today who are considered to be experiencing social, emotional or behavioural difficulties.

Oedipus' relationship with his parents was highly confusing and resulted in death and torment. Although he thought he murdered a total stranger, he had, in fact, slain his own father. Similarly, he did not discover that Jocasta was his mother until it was too late. There are many boys today whose lives and relationships are so complicated that when they become suspicious of the status quo or begin to discover the reality, it invariably leads to pain and anger towards themselves and others and often results in displays of behaviour in schools that is described as interfering with their learning and disrupting others' learning.

Similarly, there are young women who today are accused of 'leading others astray', both boys and other girls. They are usually described as 'manipulative' or 'a bad influence'. We may not refer to them as Sirens, but, nevertheless, the effect of their behaviour is deemed to be similar: to lead other young men and women away from a steady passage through life into turbulent and troubled waters.

In medieval times, a mixture of secular and religious explanations could be invoked to explain away a child's 'different' behaviour. A secular example might invoke a theory of the 'changeling'. For instance, a mother, worried that her child looked different from other children, behaved in oddly amusing or disturbing ways, or had what we might now call a physical impairment, could argue that the child was in fact not hers. She might then relate a tale of how at some moment of inattentiveness (e.g. whilst she was washing clothes at the river) gypsies or fairies had snatched her baby and left the defective child in its place.

In a more religious explanation, a man might claim that his somehow 'different' child was either the result of original sin or diabolism. Whilst the former involved a straightforward reference to the teachings of Aquinas, the second could be more colourful. If a man claimed liaison between his wife and the devil, not only might he be able to disassociate himself from his troublesome child, there was the added possibility of accusing his wife of witchcraft, with the accompanying trial and punishment that usually ended with her death.

Whilst the accusation of liaison with the devil didn't take the responsibility away from the mother and the moral turpitude argument also suggests that parents are responsible, nevertheless, the explanation served in some measure to deflect from them as the *source* of the child's behaviour. The child did not look or behave the way they did as the result of poor parenting or as the result of a hereditary genetic abnormality, but because of some external factor. Thus, the history of attitudes towards SEBD is the same as any other so-called 'abnormality'. Having absolved themselves of blame, the adults could then begin to search for some way of supporting the young person. Often, however, externalised explanations were not only used to absolve parents of blame but also of responsibility, either with their compliance or against their will.

The practice of dealing with 'difference' by conceptualising it as somehow outside or on the margins of society has continued into the present day. For example, 'society' has taken responsibility for people deemed different and chosen to remove them from the family and everyday life and contain them within institutions. A policy of containment as a way of dealing with any deviation from 'normality' permeates society. Adults who commit crime are sent to prison, people with mental ill-health can be contained in asylums and children and adults who are ill generally, can be removed to hospital. In each case, there is the assumption that once 'fixed', there can be a return to the mainstream of society.

In the past, even where the reasons for removal were not perceived as some in-child deficit, children and young people could find themselves in contexts other than their immediate family. For example, in late-nineteenth-century London, school inspectors found social deprivation and classroom behaviour similar to that reported as having a significant impact on schools today. Explanations of poverty, alcohol abuse and poor diet were seen as reasons for young people's behaviour. These explanations, in turn, served to remove any sense of blame from the child or society and allowed for the provision of support either from secular or religious charities. This model of support and the philosophical foundation that underpinned it persisted well into the twentieth century.

Charitable model – needs model – rights model

Current provision and practice in addressing the learning of young people who might be experiencing SEBD has evolved from the charitable model laid down in the late nineteenth century and this explains why much of what is done to support their learning is the way that it is today. Provision and practice in the nineteenth century, naturally, had evolved in order to meet perceived required changes in practice from previous centuries. For example, the Poor Law Act of 1597 records that a large number of 'ill-disposed children of whom the City of London was desirous to be disemburdened' were sent to the American colonies as servants. Prior to compulsory education, however, vagrant, delinquent and pauper children were usually dealt with by being sent to workhouse schools, reformatories, industrial schools or 'ragged' schools. Moreover, the large charitable families such as Cadbury and Rowntree or the Owen family in Scotland also contributed to provision, some of which continues in the present day. The children involved tended to be the children of the urban poor and again, whilst charitable measures indicate that society was taking responsibility for these troubled and troubling young people, nevertheless, in the way in which each of them was played out, we can detect a desire for society to distance itself from the behaviour of the children and, in the process, however inadvertently, by treating them differently from other children, actually distance society from the children themselves.

One explanation of the possible dichotomy between intent and actuality, might lie in a proposition that the dominant approach of both secular and religious charities was based on tolerance. The problem with tolerance is that it assumes superiority on the part of the body being tolerant towards the other, without acknowledging any sense of the 'Other' that might be equally valid. From the very outset then, charitable models are based on deficit in the other. In Scotland, and the UK as a whole, the approach adopted towards deficit was beneficence. Consequently, it was considered that the children and young people in deficit were incapable of coping with the conditions and level of work with which so-called normal children had to deal. Charitable provision reflected the hierarchical, patriarchal structures of church that were matched by the hierarchical political structures in society, and which served to reinforce each other, thus creating a hegemony that was patronising, demonising and exclusive. The obvious model of provision, therefore, was that which was already in existence elsewhere, removal from the mainstream and containment in a protected environment.

Containment was the model of provision until at least the second half of the twentieth century and it was based on the assumption that if this troublesome group could be removed from schools and classes, not only would they be better provided for, but those left in the mainstream would make better progress at a faster rate without either disturbance from their disruptive peers or the need for the teacher to spend an inordinate amount of time dealing with their learning or behaviour. Since the children and young people in protected environments were considered incapable of 'normal' work, their curriculum was usually based on a mixture of craft and physical exercise.

In the 1960s in Scotland, the provision for young people who might be experiencing social, emotional or behavioural difficulties included borstal (for young people who had offended) and approved schools. Young people could be sent to an approved school for a number of reasons including persistent absconding, violent behaviour, illness, including diabetes and epilepsy, and threatening homosexual behaviour. Even the briefest comparison with how young people in the twenty-first century are provided for indicates that even as recently as one generation ago, despite provision being founded on an admirable desire to assume responsibility, the tendency to demonise and marginalise vulnerable groups of young people was deep-rooted and strong.

As the century progressed, the charitable model and its assumption of deficit and remediation, became increasingly challenged. For example, there was a range of initiatives throughout the 1960s that called into question the remedial model of providing for the education of young people whom schools found difficult to teach. Furthermore, in an echo of the late-nine-teenth-century London inspector, some of these initiatives began to suggest that the curriculum and the nature of school may themselves be possible contributory factors towards unwanted behaviour in young learners.

Needs model and integration

This shift in thinking about how the learning of our most vulnerable young people is addressed, did not arise naturally, out of a narrow contemplation of the plight of a small percentage of young people. Rather, the discussion on provision for the learning of vulnerable groups of students was part of a wider debate on education which was itself an element of significant social change at the time. Throughout post-war Europe, a sense of freedom was accompanied by 'new' thinking and the works of writers such as Sartre and Lyotard introduced fresh ways of thinking about our world.

Consequently, the late 1970s saw the emergence of two significant reports on special education that were to impact on the nature of provision and practice for young people who at that time were described as 'maladjusted'. These reports were the Warnock Report (DES, 1978) in England and Wales, and the HMI *Progress Report* (SED, 1978) in Scotland. Most significantly, these reports challenged contemporary thinking and introduced a shift away from a charitable model based on exclusion towards a needs model based on integration.

It was Mary Warnock who coined the phrase 'special educational needs' (SEN) to replace the nine categories of handicap that were currently in use. She saw SEN as a continuum of need, in which those whose need was greatest would be educated in special schools, whilst those with minimal needs could be integrated into and taught within mainstream. The problem with integration, of course, is that it assumes a norm to which the learners in question must aspire. The idea of a norm is itself nebulous and arbitrary and the experience of most pupils in special schools was that integration into mainstream was the exception.

The HMI report in Scotland (SED 1978), similarly called into question the remedial model. Significantly, both reports also recognised that, at any one time, significant numbers of children and young people in schools would benefit from some form of support for their learning. Whilst the actual impact of these reports in terms of numbers of successful integrations might be questioned, they nevertheless introduced a sense of optimism into the context of special education and set the foundations for important changes in practice within special schools and eventually mainstream schools. In particular, by the late 1980s, there were signs of a shift away from assumptions of inadequacy and containment towards the learning of young people who might be 'maladjusted'. Indeed, it is around this time that the term 'maladjusted' was dropped in favour of the current label of 'social, emotional and behavioural difficulties' (SEBD; EBD in England and Wales). Whilst it could be argued that the new label represented no more than a change in terminology, it nevertheless recognised the range of factors that can impact upon a young person's behaviour in schools.

Rights model and inclusion

Throughout the 1990s and into the twenty-first century there has been a shift in focus away from needs and integration towards human rights and inclusion. The roots of the rights agenda in education can be found in the human rights policy emanating principally from the United Nations. In addition, in Scotland and in the Western world generally, the move towards inclusion based on human rights has been reinforced by the rise of third-way politics based on a political ideal of social inclusion (Giddens, 1994).

Consequently, the last fifteen years in Scotland has seen a range of policy and legislation aimed at the inclusion of all young people in the education system. Their impact is dealt with in greater detail in Chapter 3 but principal among them were the 1995 Children's Act, the Standards in Scotland's Schools etc. Act 2000 that introduced the presumption of mainstreaming for all young people with additional support needs, and the Additional Support for Learning Act 2004. The impact of this legislation on practice and provision resulted in the production of supporting policy documents such as *Heart of the Matter* (SCCC, 1995), and the *Code of Conduct* that followed the 2004 Act. As a result, there has been a developing impact on provision and practice throughout the 1990s and the new century on both segregated and mainstream contexts for young people who may be experiencing social, emotional or behavioural difficulties.

The impact on practice

A consideration of three recent approaches provides examples of how changing attitudes and developing understandings of children's difficulties has impacted on practice.

The first of these is the positivist approach. Positive approaches have their roots in behaviourist theories (see Chapter 2) and are typically based on systems of rewards, sanctions and token economies (Canter and Canter, 1992). These approaches are variously referred to as Positive Discipline, Assertive Discipline and Discipline with Dignity, and the basic tenet of each is pupil deficit and they are, consequently, reductionist and pessimistic in their view of young people in schools. Kohn (1996) argues that whilst positivist programmes may dress themselves up in the language of care, in action they are about control, specifically, the control of children and young people by adults; in particular, the control of pupils by teachers. Positivist approaches enjoy a measure of currency in Scottish schools. This should not be surprising as the kind of thinking that underpins this practice matches the thinking that has led to exclusive, segregated provision for young people whose behaviour schools find difficult.

In special schools and other segregated provision, positivist approaches often manifest themselves as token economies in the form of points systems. Teachers and young people often express a liking for these approaches, at least in the short term, as they are easy to operate, have some immediate impact and preserve the status quo in power relationships. However, over the longer term, for reasons explored in the other chapters, positivist approaches lose their initial impact and teachers find the same young people repeatedly referred to behaviour support.

Staged intervention approaches appear to offer another way of dealing with unwanted behaviour, at least in the early stages, where often the environment is the first consideration. For example, the Framework For Intervention (FFI) (Birmimgham, 2003) adopts a more ecological approach based on peer support for teachers. Whenever a teacher reports behavioural difficulties with a class, an environment audit is carried out, highlighting when unwanted behaviours arise and what contributes towards their manifestation. Suggestions are made with the intention of altering the environment in order to prevent the unwanted behaviour arising in the first place. If, after a short period, this proves to be ineffective, only then will the focus turn towards individual pupils. Crucially, however, there is recognition at this stage that the child or young person does not exist only in school and parents, carer and guardians are invited to contribute towards and take part in whatever support measures are developed. At the third stage, the support network widens to include other agencies such as psychological services and social work, if they are not already involved.

Whilst the Framework still contains elements of deficit-laden, positivist approaches (it is still the teacher who decides that behaviour is 'unwanted' and who identifies individuals as having behavioural difficulties) there is, nevertheless, recognition that, whatever one may believe about young people's inherent dispositions, the environment has a significant impact on their behaviour. Moreover, 'environment' is understood to mean more than the immediate classroom context, but also the home and the community.

Notwithstanding some of the difficulties with the introduction of the Framework, it offers a shift away from a focus solely on pupil deficit towards a consideration of the wider school and community context. In particular, the thinking behind the Framework recognises that the relationship between behaviour and learning is a significant factor in the construction of behavioural difficulties in schools (Birmingham, 2003).

Approaches to dealing with young people's behaviour that take the relationship between behaviour and learning as their starting point, tend to argue that social, emotional and behavioural difficulties constitute a learning difficulty in much the same way as any other learning difficulty (Head and O'Neill, 1999; Head, 2005). Crucially, however, they argue that the starting point for dealing with difficulties is not the young person's behaviour, but their learning. Developments from such programmes, therefore, suggest that simply aiming at the reduction or eradication of undesirable behaviour is, in itself, inadequate. Instead, teachers should be looking to develop learning behaviour in all their pupils (Head, 2005). However, a consideration of the origins of these approaches again reveals that they are based on assumptions of deficit. For example, Feuerstein's Instrumental Enrichment (IE) is posited on a list of deficient cognitive functions and his programme aims to develop these through a range of cognitive modalities. Similarly, thinking skills' approaches to learning (Fisher, 1999, 2000; Lipman, 1988, 1993, 2003; McGuiness, 1999) are based on assumptions of cognitive deficiency.

However, each of the three approaches offers hope that thinking may be shifting. The very existence of positivist approaches in schools is a recognition that young learners require more than support for their subject knowledge. Despite arguments that insist that such approaches may, in fact, serve to reinforce the behaviour they are trying to eliminate, there is nevertheless a tacit recognition that there is a relationship between behaviour and learning and that one impacts on the other. Environmentalists and educationalists who subscribe to approaches that focus on learning, whilst still posited on deficit, offer another way of dealing with that deficit. Basically, instead of attempting to eradicate the deficit, they offer opportunities to nurture young people as effective learners.

The impact on provision

Within the special sector, developments since the early 1990s have seen the introduction of a more formal curriculum in residential and day schools. Prior to this development, the priority for special schools dealing with 'maladjusted' children and young people was a focus on their behaviour and its causes. As a consequence of their difficulty in adjusting to the accepted social norms of behaviour, there was an assumption that either they were not capable of the level of intellectual engagement demanded by the mainstream curriculum or that it was not a priority for them. As a result, the curriculum tended to consist mostly of informal activities, with the formal being limited largely to literacy, mathematics, physical education and vocational subjects at a relatively low level. However, the impact of the rights agenda resulted in special schools for children and young people who might be experiencing social, emotional or behavioural difficulties adopting a more formal curriculum, with pupils able to access national examinations. At the same time, special provision for the same young people appeared to diminish as many local authorities closed their own residential schools. In addition, throughout this time, there has been a movement towards closer working between education and social work, resulting in the advent of jointly or social work run day centres providing education for young people who have been excluded from mainstream schools.

The impact on provision and practice in mainstream schools has been equally significant. Principally, there has been an expansion of small-scale support in the form of bases and units either belonging solely to a school or supporting pupils from a cluster of schools. Within bases and units, teachers are developing the skills, approaches and philosophies required to support children within the context of inclusion (see, for example, Head and Jamieson (2006)). Within mainstream classes themselves, a series of initiatives such as the FFI and others aimed at positive behaviour in classrooms have been introduced as ways of supporting teachers to deal with the behaviour of difficult pupils. As a result, the profile of provision for children with behavioural difficulties in Scotland ranges from secure provision for children who have committed serious crimes or are in danger of harming themselves or others to meeting the needs of all children in mainstream schools. It can be argued, therefore, that whilst some of the provision represents the development of an increasingly optimistic view of difficult young people, nevertheless the tendency to patronise, demonise and marginalise still remains.

Secure provision

Although children usually arrive in secure provision through the courts or the children's hearing system in Scotland, it should be remembered that secure units are not part of the penal system but are an element of the care and education of young people who have offended or who are at risk. In Scotland, most of the secure units are run by the Catholic Church. The educational provision within such an establishment typically mirrors that of mainstream schools but in reduced or amended form. In addition, (at least in some secure establishments) school is compulsory, even for young people beyond the statutory school leaving age. The young people in secure provision will be presented for award-bearing courses similar to their peers in other educational contexts. A student, therefore, is likely to be offered the opportunity to take modular and/or Scottish Qualification Authority (SQA) courses and their route through these is usually detailed in a personal development plan or individualised education plan. This ensures that the young person's academic, intellectual and personal interests are met through the educational element of secure provision.

However, given the troubled background of many of the young people in such provision, the principal aim of secure provision is to enable them to develop the skills and attributes necessary to form positive and effective relationships that will both enable them to take maximum advantage of the opportunities offered them and to engage positively with society when they leave. Consequently, the educational programme may contain elements of cognitive and affective development in addition to the more traditional subjects of language, maths, science, home economics and information and computing technology (ICT).

Education is only one (albeit a major) element of secure provision. Consequently, secure units are staffed by both teachers and care staff who work together to ensure the young people's welfare and personal development.

Residential schools

Residential schools can, in many respects, be similar to secure provision but without the secure element. Young people in such schools usually find themselves there because they have been unable to cope with mainstream schools or vice versa. The usual route is through a local authority's educational needs assessment system, probably staffed by psychological services and social work as well as education staff. Many authorities in Scotland have reduced or eliminated this type of provision from their range, and those residential schools which remain are largely in the independent sector. Most residential schools also have a significant number of day pupils among their population.

Again, the curriculum is likely to be a reduced version of that on offer within mainstream education and will include programmes aimed at helping young people to overcome their difficulties. Residential schools also, where possible, work closely with parents in trying to create the home environment that will allow the young person to return successfully to the community.

Once more, residential schools are staffed by teaching and care staff. Additionally, there is often a significant input from social work services in such environments.

Special day-schools

Day-school provision for young people with SEBD is usually within the pupil's local authority. As with secure and residential provision, the education programmes are likely to be abridged and amended versions of mainstream curricula and children will be presented for SQA exams, National

Tests and other awards. Again, there will be elements of cognitive and affective development as part of the young person's development and educational plans in special school contexts. Referral to psychological services and the authority's assessment procedures is the usual way in which a student will find himself or herself in a special school.

A typical school of this type will cater for between twenty and thirty children and the teacher–pupil ratio is usually 1:6. Non-teaching staff are likely to consist of one or two auxiliaries and administrative staff.

The clear focus on attainment, the small class sizes and the range of programmes provided are the main advantages of special provision. In these circumstances, it is argued that educational and personal programmes can be tailored to ensure that young people are able to sustain their lives within their local community and, where appropriate, to prepare themselves for the next stage in their development whether that be the move from primary to secondary school, a return to mainstream education or preparation for leaving school.

Secondary special schools are likely to have close contact with a number of Further Education (FE) colleges which provide the kind of vocational courses which are often deemed to be attractive to their students, and which offer a means of bridging from school to the world of work.

Off-site bases and units

The crucial difference between this type of provision and that just described is that children attending bases and units normally remain on the role of their mainstream school and attend on a part-time basis. Such bases often service a number of schools and the curricula and programmes offered vary in response to the length of time the young person works within the base, the nature of the young person's difficulties and the most appropriate programme for the child as agreed by the young person, their parents, their school and unit or base staff. Generally speaking, the shorter the time the student spends within the base, the smaller the subject element and the deeper the concentration on addressing their behavioural difficulties.

In order to do this, base staff often work very closely with pupils, parents, colleagues in mainstream schools and other professionals in social work and psychological services. Typically, a pupil might be in S1 or S2 and attend the base two or three times a week for a duration somewhere between a double period and a half day on each occasion (although it should be noted that what happens between authorities and among bases within the same authority can vary widely). Whilst there, the student might participate in group and individual work aimed at supporting them through their personal development, as well as subject work, perhaps within an area of the curriculum in which the pupil is experiencing particular difficulty.

Mainstream provision

With the move towards inclusion, many schools now find themselves developing new and interesting methods of supporting young people within mainstream provision. Often this is done through the setting up of an in-school base where children who may be experiencing difficulties can either choose to go or may be referred by teaching staff. In addition, some authorities have appointed a teacher in each school whose specific remit is to manage and develop strategies for supporting young people and staff in schools.

In primary schools, this may include the use of peripatetic behaviour support staff who visit schools on a regular basis to work with particular pupils, classes and colleagues. In secondary schools, behaviour support is part of the range of provision aimed at supporting all pupils in their intellectual, personal and social development. This provision would include guidance and learning support in addition to the school's systems, structures and policy for dealing with students' difficulties.

Regardless of context or what takes place in all of the provision just described, there is an underpinning assumption that the young people who attend are somehow in deficit and require something different from their peers in order to eliminate unwanted behaviour. Moreover, whether provision is on-site within mainstream or separate, there is a shared supposition that, whether for short or extended periods, some students need to be separated from their peers. The reasons offered as justification range from depicting the pupil as disruptive to claims of altruism asserting that the pupil's needs would be better met elsewhere. The provision made within the mainstream, and for students who remain on the role of their mainstream school, nevertheless retains elements of exclusion based on beliefs that construct them as variously troublesome or vulnerable and serve to marginalise their learning. It can be argued, therefore, that the impact of recent developments in provision has been to replicate the exclusionary 'special' system, with albeit a more optimistic version, within the mainstream.

Smith (2006) argues that there are two reasons for provision developing in this way. The first concerns the condition of education generally. Education in Scotland, Smith claims, is dominated by a reductionist paradigm that has its roots in an assumption of deficit and disability (Poplin, 1988).

The second reason stems from the fact that the inclusion movement has its roots in special education. From the outset, UNESCO policy (for example, UNESCO, 1994) has concentrated on the movement of learners from special contexts into mainstream schools, thereby reinforcing the notion that inclusion is about what is done to protect the rights and welfare of particular groups of learners. The effect of this line of thought is to keep educationalists' collective focus firmly on the special sector, to interrogate, question and critique separate provision and to argue that justice lies in moving learners into mainstream. Consequently:

In Scotland, the evolution of the education system has revolved around where rather than how children should be educated, so the movement of children from special educational settings into mainstream provision is not a new phenomenon. (Smith, 2006, p. 7)

Inevitably, the move towards inclusion has led to tensions and contradictions (Dyson, 2001). In the special sector, for instance, it is provision and practice that have been called into question and inclusion seen as the answer (Head *et al.*, 2003; Kane *et al.*, 2004). By way of contrast, in mainstream, it is inclusion itself, especially the inclusion of children and young people who may be experiencing social, emotional and behavioural difficulties that has been blamed for perceived rises in indiscipline and a negative impact on levels of attainment (Munn *et al.*, 2004; Pirrie *et al.*, 2005; Wilkin *et al.*, 2006). Since the voice of the mainstream is louder, it has come to dominate thinking among practitioner teachers in Scotland, thereby reinforcing an unquestioned hegemony of the mainstream.

Hogan (2005, p. 83) explains that this kind of thinking is indicative of a 'conclusive theory of human nature' in which learner identity, which may be variously optimistic or pessimistic, is constructed in terms of that theory and that it is currently enjoying popularity and competes with other similarly 'conclusive' theories for authority and influence. He further argues that whilst such theories might claim a toleration of diversity, it is nevertheless 'informed and circumscribed by a more important emphasis on uniformity' (Hogan, 2005, p. 83) and that uniformity is achieved through the imposition of a prescribed and unchallenged curriculum. Thus the practices that evolve from such contexts tend to reinforce notions of normativity, the rightness of mainstream, and learner identity as that which fits with the compliant, studious mainstream pupil. The 'special' pupil, especially the learner who may be experiencing social, emotional or behavioural difficulties, does not fit easily into that mould and, therefore, represents a challenge to the mainstream system.

Opponents of the inclusion of young people who may be experiencing behavioural difficulties argue that whilst inclusion is admirable, it is a political ideal and that there is no evidence base to show that it 'works'. Thomas and Glenny (2005) challenge that position as itself a political argument posited on a particular set of beliefs that might resonate with Poplin's reductionist paradigm (Poplin, 1988). Instead, they argue, that if we are to generate deeper understanding of inclusion:

we have to take a new stance towards our practices. Instead of just living in them and taking their implicit construal of things as they are, we have to understand how they have come to be, how they come to embed a certain view of things. (Thomas and Glenny, 2005, p. 10)

The 'certain view of things' that is the subject of this book is the nature of social emotional and behavioural difficulties as they are embedded in the perceptions of teachers, schools and society in a wider sense, and the provision that we make for them as a consequence.

Chapter 2

THEORIES OF BEHAVIOUR AND THE CONSTRUCTION OF THE SEBD CHILD

Pupils, teachers and school managers hold a range of views on classroom behaviour and how (if at all) it should be supported. The views that they hold can be understood and explained by a range of theories relating to behaviour and learning. Likewise, the interactions between pupils and teachers can be understood by reference to the same theories. The discussion in this chapter relies on the work of Ayers, *et al.* (2000), Head and Jamieson (2006), Head, *et al.* (2003), Kane, *et al.* (2004), Macleod (2006) and Porter (2000).

First of all, it might be helpful to consider what is meant by theory and what a theory is. At a very basic level, to theorise is simply to think about something. However, in addition to this loose and speculative activity, there are also well-thought out and articulated theories. For example, Piaget's and Vygotsky's theories on learning inform the basis of education throughout the Western world. They are the result of years of academic rigour and have been the subject of thorough research. In this instance, the theories are founded on psychological beliefs about how humans, especially young people, learn.

Another set of beliefs that lead to theories of behaviour are based on biology. The underlying belief is that genetic, neurological and physiological processes influence behaviour. A theory based on this belief might advocate that behavioural difficulties are addressed through medication and therapy.

Although not largely acknowledged within the literature on social, emotional and behavioural difficulties, each of the theories is informed by a philosophy. Indeed, Porter (2000, p. 10) argues that the sets of beliefs held by teachers about children and their behaviour can be informed by personal philosophical positions or philosophies of education and behaviour that have a much wider adherence.

Whatever the philosophical, psychological or social origins of a theory, they all help to explain and generate understanding of the world in which we live and operate. Theories of learning and theories of behaviour, therefore, help us to make sense of what we do with and for children as part of their learning. Like most theories current in education, those described by Porter and Ayers *et al.* tend to concentrate on psychology. Porter (2000) argues that theories can be categorised broadly as being on a continuum that runs from authoritarian at one end to authoritative and democratic at the other. The language used here is interesting as both terms describe a relationship between learner and teacher that is based upon power. Even within those democratic theories of humanism, choice theory and systems theory, the teacher is the powerful party. It is the teacher who has the ability to 'facilitate' learning and to create the conditions in which students' learning meets their intellectual, social and emotional needs; it is the teacher who can make it possible for the student to make better choices; and it is the teacher who is able to change student–teacher relationships by altering their interactions with students. In each of these approaches, the teacher is the one who instigates action to address behaviour and the student is essentially passive, at least up to that point. In this chapter, theories of behaviour and learning and how they relate to the provision and practice for young people who might be experiencing social, emotional and behavioural difficulties are considered under three broad headings of behaviourist theories, humanist theories and systems theories.

Behaviourist theories

Behavioural approaches to providing for pupils experiencing social, emotional and behavioural difficulties are based on the same principle of behaviourism that informs didactic styles of teaching. That is, that all behaviour is learned and, therefore, can be unlearned. Consequently, its main thrust is to concentrate on the manifestations of behaviour; to focus on unacceptable behaviours that are observable and measurable and to reduce their frequency or replace them with acceptable behaviours. In its pure, theoretical form, there is little or no consideration of the causes of behaviours.

Typically, a school using this approach will make high use of behaviour contracts and systems of rewarding good behaviour, whilst the consequence for poor behaviour will be some form of sanction or punishment. Frequently, these behaviours will be targeted, with say, a pupil being rewarded for saying 'please' but sanctioned for swearing whilst other behaviours do not receive the same focus.

One of the main advantages of a behaviourist approach is that it is easily understood by both teachers and pupils. In the example given above, both know the behaviour which is to be nurtured and can look for opportunities for pupils to use it. Likewise, pupil and teacher are both aware of the target behaviour to be avoided and the punishment or sanction to be applied when it is displayed. Similarly, the rewards for good behaviour are usually decided beforehand. As a result, this method takes up little of the teacher's time and is relatively inexpensive to operate. There is no need for additional staff or resources and, since the focus is on the behaviour and not the child, there is no need to involve other agencies thereby ensuring that staff time spent on dealing with the problem is kept to a minimum. It establishes very tight boundaries for behaviour and can, it is argued, help make the world less puzzling and threatening for pupils. Consequently, behaviourism is common in approaches used, for example, for pupils with autism.

The main disadvantages of this approach are that it can be mechanistic and short term. Whilst the clear statement of behaviours, sanctions and rewards is easy to follow, it diminishes the importance of the element of human interaction necessary for the development of relationships. The rewards are extrinsic, are granted by the teacher, and as they lose their sense of novelty, become ineffective. There is generally little attempt to foster intrinsic motivation, as this would involve more staff time. Consequently, any improvements in behaviour are unlikely to be internalised or to be long term. Furthermore, there are ethical questions surrounding this approach. In adopting a behaviourist methodology (whether as a short-term or long-term approach) the place of children's rights can be marginalised: for example, the right to grow up making mistakes and the right to dissent are often suppressed rather than channelled in an appropriate direction. In particular, it can also be argued that a behaviourist approach can jeopardise the operation of free will by imposing behaviours on children rather than nurturing socially acceptable behaviour. Moreover, it can be argued that a system of agreed behaviours and consequences disempowers teachers who might otherwise choose to handle the situation in a more individualistic way. A criticism arising from this argument is that striving for consistency replaces creativity. A more immediate criticism, however, might be that concentration on the behaviour itself, rather than the context that leads to that behaviour, ignores opportunities to resolve an unwanted situation. Nevertheless, behaviourist theories have dominated the understanding of the nature of behavioural difficulties and the provision for young people who are considered to be difficult.

The Education Act of 1872 saw the establishment of public schools in Britain. From the very beginning, however, it was recognised that there were young people for whom this was not an entirely enriching experience. This was interpreted as being the result of their inability to function within the system and it was asserted that their presence in schools interfered with the smooth running of the education system. As indicated in Chapter 1, the favoured way of dealing with difficult children in the nineteenth century was to remove them to a series of workhouses and charitable schools in England and industrial schools and reform schools in Scotland, hence the model of marginalised, segregated provision. However, child-deficit was not the only interpretation of the context and removal from the state system was not universally accepted as the solution. A London school inspector in the 1890s remarked that 'dull and naughty children are manufactured by the cast-iron requirements of modern education codes', with the implication that changes in these codes would help eradicate the difficulties. There are two significant points that emerge from this statement that can be made regarding the development of the educational experience of young learners. Firstly, had this argument become prevalent our schools would have developed quite differently in response to children's social, emotional and behavioural difficulties. Secondly, it shows that the concept that difficulties may have their roots within the system itself (and not simply within-child), is not new; such thinking has a pedigree at least as long as the exclusionist view and prefigures similar concerns in the 1978 HMI *Progress Report* in Scotland (SED, 1978).

Noting the existence of differing strands in thinking about social, emotional and behavioural difficulties introduces an element of complexity in our conceptualisation of the term as a legitimate descriptive category of learners. Adopting simplistic explanations of SEBD such as child/teacher/curriculum/system deficit becomes questionable and it may be more helpful to adopt an overview that endeavours to see the implications of all of these elements for the educational experience of children and young people who may be experiencing social, emotional or behavioural difficulties.

However, throughout the twentieth century the favoured method of dealing with difficult children remained that of removing them from mainstream schools in order that the education of 'normal' children should not suffer. For example, the Education (Scotland) Act of 1962 allowed for 'education by special methods appropriate to the special requirements of pupils who suffer from disability of mind or body'. This, as one might expect, led to a massive increase in provision of what in Scotland were called 'list G' schools and a consequent increase (estimated by some to be in the region of 150%) in the number of children identified as 'maladjusted' between 1960 and 1976. The range of provision described in Chapter 1 indicates that, with relatively minor adjustments, this remains the profile of provision today.

Alongside a concern about what to do with difficult children has been a parallel search for appropriate terminology that allows for the identification and assessment of difficult learners. The Idiots Act of 1886 is an example of this struggle. Within the Act, idiocy was defined as a greater deficiency of intellect, and imbecility as a lesser degree of such deficiency. The vagueness of the definitions reflects, perhaps, a struggle to understand exactly what the terms mean whilst acknowledging some commonly held sense of personal or pathological deficiency. In the twentieth century the terminology may have changed, but it nevertheless remained firmly rooted in the language of defect. Terms such as 'maladjusted' and 'handicap' have fallen out of use, but more recent terms such as 'SEN' and 'support for learning' and even the current 'additional support needs', still contain an element of presumed deficit.

In 1947 the Advisory Council on Education in Scotland was empowered by the Secretary of State to review the provision made in Scotland for the education of children, 'who suffer from disability of mind or body or from maladjustment due to social handicaps'. This last category firmly places children whom we would now consider to be experiencing and/or exhibiting social, emotional or behavioural difficulties within the sphere of medicine. This was followed by the Education (Scotland) Act of 1954 which gave local authorities the right to recruit the medical profession in the process of ascertainment, including the 'diagnosis' of behavioural difficulties. Thus, the neuropathic child of the first half of the century became the maladjusted pupil of post-war education. 'Maladjusted' remained in common use as a descriptor of children experiencing difficulty at least until the late 1980s in Scotland.

The Warnock Report (DES, 1978) recommended that the various categories of handicap should be replaced by the single generic category of SEN. Children thus identified were to have these needs addressed, thereby allowing them to be reintegrated into mainstream education. This report was influential in changing the focus from medicine towards education and the recognition that educational measures could be taken to address children's needs.

Although the medical model is deemed a thing of the past, and ascertainment by the medical profession has been replaced by assessment by psychologists and teachers, there nevertheless remains a movement towards physiological explanations of behaviour. Thus recent years have seen an increase in the diagnosis of children's behaviour in terms of medical/psychological terminology such as 'autism', 'attention deficit disorder', 'attention deficit hyperactivity disorder', 'Asperger's syndrome' and 'dyspraxia' with, in some cases, medication being prescribed in order to keep the child 'balanced' and calm. The increase in the number of pupils attracting one of these labels is so great that it is entirely possible that their use may, in fact, lead to the relegation of SEBD as the favoured term for this group of young people.

The desire to seek such explanations may originate from the effect that it appears to reassure parents that their children's difficulties are not the result of 'bad' parenting but are the result of illness or a condition. This was encapsulated in Lord Elton's 1989 attempt at defining what we now call social, emotional and behavioural difficulties as 'severe and persistent behaviour problems as a result of emotional , psychological or neurological disturbance'. The overwhelming thrust of such explanations is to assert that the problems lie within the child rather than the child's interactions with others, within the school system itself, and/or within the construction and content of the curriculum. Therefore, in similar fashion to previous generations described in Chapter 1, the effect of adopting medical or quasi-medical explanations is to distance adults and society from the perceived causal circumstances, thereby exonerating them from any blame for the child's behaviour.

Humanist theories

Humanist theories of behaviour are posited on the belief that learners will learn when what they are learning matches their cognitive and affective needs. The teacher's task is to help pupils become aware of their intellectual and emotional needs and to help them extend any restrictions to their needs, for example, seeing no point in learning whatever is being taught. Implied within these theories, therefore, is the assumption that when conditions are as just described little or no disruptive behaviour will occur. When it does arise, it should be solved through discussion and negotiation, perhaps in a manner to that outlined below as reconciling competing narratives.

Like behaviourist theories, humanist theories of behaviour maintain a focus on the child and, unsurprisingly, therefore, a psychodynamic approach can be informed by these theories. This approach has its roots in the work of Freud. Its proponents see the origin of problem behaviour in the unconscious or subconscious thoughts of the child as a result of experiences in early childhood. It follows, therefore, that in order to explain behaviours, pupils' life histories need to be reviewed so that their inner world of emotions can be reconciled with the outer world.

Counselling, therefore, is the approach most appropriate to this model. Given its roots in Freud, presumably a psychoanalytical approach would be the first choice. Recently, however, some person-centred approaches to counselling have become more popular and can be adapted for use by non-specialists such as teachers. An example of this would be Solution Focused Brief Therapy (George *et al.*, 1999). Such approaches encourage children to explore their inner feelings and resources and are non-judgemental, respectful and dignified for the child. Support for younger children that can be understood in psychodynamic terms is exemplified in the use of nurture groups. Within these groups, a profile is developed that guides adults towards helping children learn what they should have learned or experienced as very young children, for example, trust in adults (Bennathan and Boxall, 2000).

The most obvious advantage of this approach is that it is pupil-centred. Consequently, the purpose and effect of this approach is to empower the pupil to develop his or her own strategies for overcoming unacceptable behaviour. This is achieved through developing an understanding of why specific behaviours happen in particular contexts, and by nurturing those strategies that they already employ effectively. As a result of solutions being generated by the learner, it is argued that changes in behaviour are more likely to be permanent and the overall effect longer rather than shorter term.

The most obvious disadvantage of this approach is that it can be very time-consuming both in terms of professional input (from a teacher or counsellor) and in effecting change. If teachers are to be the counsellors, this has implications for staff development and is dependent on the degree to which any given teacher feels confident in entering into the world of children's emotions. Again there are ethical questions. Since this involves a significant degree of teacher input is it right that teachers are taken from their prime purpose in order to take part in this approach? Likewise, since there is no guaranteed success, is it acceptable to use up both the students' and teachers' time in this way?

In England and Wales, as we have noted, the term 'emotional and behavioural difficulties' replaced that of 'maladjusted'. The terminology reflects the language of psychology in the identification and assessment of these difficulties. In Scotland, the term was expanded to include social difficulties, thus recognising the role of society beyond school in both the creation and solution of children's difficulties. The crucial difference between these two approaches can, perhaps, be highlighted by an account of a short session within a video conference held recently by one Scottish local authority (Case study 1).

Case study 1

In this session, the speaker (a professor from an American university) compared the behaviours of different groups of teenagers. In America, for example, he told his audience, a significant number of disputes between teenagers result in death. This compares unfavourably with teenage disputes in Canada, another North American country with many cultural similarities and pressures for young people. The crucial difference, he maintained, is that in America it is legal to carry firearms. As a result, many American teenagers carry guns and, not surprisingly, use them to settle violent disputes.

He also compared the experiences of parents of young people in mainstream American society with those in the Amish community. Both sets of parents complain that they are concerned about the rebellious nature of their children's behaviour. However, whilst the mainstream parent might be referring to the misuse of alcohol, drugs and violence, the Amish parent might complain of their child wearing a brightly coloured shirt or taking a lift in a car.

The point the speaker was making here is that it is a natural propensity among young people to 'rebel' against perceived social norms. In a comparison of the examples given above, however, it is clear that children will misbehave only as far as their culture and society allows them to misbehave. In other words, in terms of his example, social, emotional and behavioural difficulties are not a medical or psychological 'condition' but a social construct. If this is the case, then the question of who is considered to 'have' social, emotional or behavioural difficulties, and how they are constructed, becomes increasingly complex. The example does not deny, in fact in its narrative acknowledges, the contribution that social and emotional factors play in young people's behaviour. However, the behaviour itself only becomes 'difficult' when it is perceived to be so by wider society. The settling of disputes by the taking of human life is acceptable in most societies under certain circumstances, the most obvious being war. In most other instances, however, the same act is punishable by law. The example also indicates that what is considered unacceptable behaviour is dependent upon the culture in which the behaviour takes place and the person who is judging it. Consequently, as the illustration of the concerns to two different sets of parents indicates, what is perceived by one observer to be serious misbehaviour may well be thought by another to be a minor indiscretion.

If social, emotional and behavioural difficulties can be considered as a continuum, then at one end might be acting out behaviour that manifests itself in aggression and violence, with withdrawn behaviour at the other end (Cooper, 1996). In between these extremes might typically be found truancy, minor crime such as theft, constant low-level disruption and irritation, eating disorders, hyperactivity and social and interpersonal skills difficulties. This list could be expanded to include the aforementioned relatively recently created categories of autism, attention deficit disorder, attention deficit hyperactivity disorder and Asperger's syndrome. The growth in categories over recent years reflects two important aspects of working with young learners: first, the desire to understand behavioural difficulties and the wish to be more effective in teaching children who display them; and secondly, the problem of defining social, emotional and behavioural difficulties as a coherent category of learner. The twin aspects of this struggle are neatly articulated in the following 'definition':

> By definition, children who are called maladjusted or disturbed attract these labels because they have disturbed adults. The adults' disturbance may be at the level of frustration or anxiety at not 'getting through to' the child, or it may be sheer physical fear of violence. The term 'disturbing' implies a recognition of the children's effects on adults while the terms 'maladjusted' and 'disturbed' are too often taken to imply psychological or social characteristics in the child. (Galloway & Goodwin, 1987, p. 15)

In Galloway and Goodwin's definition, the recognition of the social nature of social emotional and behavioural difficulties is clearly seen. It is only a difficulty because it appears in a certain social context (the school) and is problematic because it is the result of the interaction among people (pupils and teachers) and is judged by at least one of these groups (teachers and some pupils) to be disturbing or disruptive. Also in this definition, the desire to pin some psychological, medical or pseudo-medical label on difficult children is recognised.

However, the situation may be more complex than this. There are other points of view, which argue that in order to understand and support children with social, emotional or behavioural difficulties, it is necessary to look beyond the school and consider the child's position in the family and wider community. It is possible that school children from poor, working-class backgrounds are more likely to be considered as having behavioural difficulties. Likewise, it may be that age and gender are important factors in identifying pupils who are constructed as having social, emotional or behavioural difficulties (Lloyd, 2005). Finally, even at the level of the classroom, the defining and identification of behavioural difficulties is not a simplistic matter. The ethos of the school, of classrooms, the nature of teacher–pupil interactions, and the tolerance level of teachers are important factors in the identification of the difficulties themselves.

What can be implied from the above description is that defining social, emotional and behavioural difficulties is an essential step in creating a deeper understanding of the educational experience of children who attract the label. So far the definitions of social, emotional and behavioural difficulties are rather unsophisticated, but perhaps the one vital element identified is that even considering all possible contributory factors (the child, the school, the curriculum, the community) there is a clear sense that SEBD (because it is a label given by teachers and some pupils to other children) is a social construct.

Children often complain of unfairness and inconsistency either from particular teachers or across the school. Likewise, teaching colleagues often complain that the way with which behavioural difficulties are dealt is unfair (on themselves and other pupils) and inconsistent (in comparison with how they or another pupil would be treated if they behaved similarly). The suggestion being made here is that the dichotomy in perception arises out of different interpretations of the social context in which the behaviour is taking place. One way of gaining an appreciation of how dichotomies are created is to consider the notion of narrative (Bruner, 1996) and its importance in producing insight into what is taking place within any social context. Within any given social context, there are likely to be dominant and personal narratives. In schools, there may be a hierarchy of narratives so that the narrative of the education system dominates that of school managers, who in turn provide the dominant narrative for the school population. The personal narratives are those that communicate the everyday experiences of school managers, teachers and pupils as they relate to the school system. In the relationship between teachers and pupils it is the teacher's narrative, in as much as it reflects the concerns of the education system and the school, that is dominant.

When dominant and personal narratives dovetail then there are likely to be few problems. When dominant and personal narratives are at odds with each other then difficulties are more likely to be encountered. All pupils in all types of schools will have personal narratives. Pupils whose personal narratives appear not to clash with the dominant narrative of school and the education system will be less likely to encounter difficulties as they progress through school. However, for learning support and behaviour support teachers, it is often the pupil whose personal narrative is at odds with the dominant narrative that is the pupil with whom they work. Outlined below (Case study 2) is a personal narrative for a pupil who encountered difficulties in school.

Case study 2

Jack came to his behaviour base one day complaining that he had been treated unfairly. 'I was the only one who did what I was told', he said, 'and I got into trouble for it. The teacher went out of the room and told us all to get on with our work while he was away. When he went out we were throwing bits of paper and rubber at each other and making a noise. We were all doing it. When he came back in he said anyone who had been throwing things should just own up now. All the others just sat down but I stood up and he gave me a row and a puni[shment exercise].'

The narrative from the teacher's perspective
'I had to go out of the room for a couple of minutes so I told them to get on with their work and behave. They're not a bad class but I knew they wouldn't. When I came back, I told them that I knew what they had been up to and those responsible should just own up now. I didn't really mean it and expected the usual response of everyone settling to their work and no one admitting they had misbehaved. However, when I looked up, there was Jack standing up. Some of the others were giggling and I think he was enjoying the attention. When I asked him why he was standing up, he said that he had been throwing bits of rubber which caused even more laughter. I'm not sure if he was being challenging or just trying to have a laugh at my expense so I just gave him a punishment exercise and told him to sit down and get on with his work. I didn't want to make a big deal out of it.'

Whilst these are rather simplistic (and could rightly be accused of being stereotypical) examples of competing narratives, they demonstrate the kind of social contexts that can be created and that serve to construct some pupils as having behavioural difficulties. The example also highlights the misunderstanding and the mismatch of expectations that can occur. In this instance, the young person had a history of behaviours that suggested he may well have been somewhere on the Autistic Spectrum, albeit, with a very mild form of disorder, and, in this instance he understood the teacher's command in literal terms. Had the teacher known this, he may well have dealt with the pupil in a quite different way. Understanding how and where differences in perception manifest themselves and working with pupils to overcome them can bring the personal and dominant narratives closer together. Narrative then, is important when supporting learning.

Teachers working within behaviour support contexts often feel that they need (and are expected) to solve all the difficulties that children present in school and beyond. However, if the context is understood from the perspective of differing narratives, then the task takes on a clearer focus: that of bringing competing narratives closer together to the point where they become mutually understandable and acceptable. A humanist approach, therefore, might include seeking ways of reconciling competing narratives.

Systems theories

Unlike other theories of behaviour, systems theories do not focus on children per se but on the environment that surrounds them, in particular the interactions between teachers and pupils. A systems approach would also recognise that a problem in school is liable to be manifest in other areas of a student's life and that addressing the problem is not the function of school alone.

Garner & Gains (1996) argument in their account of this approach is that all children belong to a set of subsystems and that behaviour is a product of interaction among and within these subsystems. Problem behaviour, therefore, is considered such because it originates in and constitutes dysfunction among these subsystems. The strategies employed are likely to be whole-school, multi agency, and intra- and inter- professional.

Within this approach there is a clear recognition that since the effects of dysfunction can be found in a number of areas of the child's life then influences and factors from each of these areas are likely to be significant in achieving progress for the child. As such, the child, his or her parents, and professionals and other interested parties from beyond the school are likely to be involved in this approach. The overview in an ecosystemic approach, if for no other reason than the involvement of a range of people, is much more holistic than in the other approaches. Moreover, since the dysfunction is perceived to be systemic, there is less focus on the 'within-child' explanation of the other approaches, thus removing much of the 'heat' from emotional and behavioural difficulties. Lastly, since each of the subsystems are interdependent, then improvement in one area is more likely to have an effect in other areas of the child's life.

The main disadvantage of an ecosystemic approach is that, at least under current circumstances in Scotland, it can be difficult to arrange.

Moreover, real collaboration among professionals can be elusive as, at least initially, they come to the learner with their own points of view and different approaches and agendas. It follows that an ecosystemic approach is liable to be time-consuming and expensive in terms of organisation, professional involvement and staff development and training.

The impact of theories

Whichever theory or combination of theories best explains and help us understand a learning context will impact on how teachers think about and react to the behaviour of the young people with whom they work. In addition, personally held views and theories form part of teachers' professional identity and they bring that identity to the context of the school. The school context, teacher identity and personal experiences and backgrounds create a set of assumptions that determine how pupils and their behaviour are viewed. Matthews (2006) argues that situations are viewed

> through the veil of a set of cultural assumptions and modes of thinking. These give rise to a set of categorizations of other people. These categories . . . are often the source of oppression and dislike. (p. 23)

Maclcod (2006) argues that deep set values of Scottish society have resulted in the experience of young people whom schools consider to be difficult to be one of punishment rather than welfare and that

> individual failure is the responsibility of the individual [and consequently] . . . within such a system if a pupil appears disengaged or to be having difficulties of some kind it is less likely that attention will focus on the system as a possible cause. (p. 158)

Similarly, Kane *et al.* (2004) found that regardless of the fact that some schools described their provision as being part of pastoral care and support, the young people involved saw it as punishment and part of the discipline system.

This may be the general experience of young people who have exhibited difficult behaviour in Scottish schools, but equally, of course, teachers' beliefs and assumptions can lead to a more optimistic point of view. Consequently, a teacher holding a pessimistic view of children and whose practice can be understood in terms of behaviourist theories of behaviour may well fit Matthews' description, whilst a teacher with a more optimistic view of learners in a context in which more humanist theories of behaviour are dominant is likely see children differently. Such a teacher, moreover, is likely to acknowledge the differences between individual students and, rather than suppress them, will acknowledge them as part of students' identities and work with them.

The creation of a category of learners with the SEBD label emanates from and reinforces behaviourist principles. Belief in a category is under-pinned by a set of assumptions about the members of that category. Most important is the belief that the major way in which learners categorised as having or displaying social, emotional or behavioural difficulties differ from their peers is in the manifestation of their behaviour as it is perceived by the observer (in this case the teacher). This disguises the ways in which pupils in schools have more in common with each other than separates them. Indeed, the SEBD category itself becomes a negative marker of difference that suppresses the acknowledgement of other differences that may be significant and/or positive. For example, the category inhibits considera-tion of possibly different experiences of female and male students, of the changing circumstances of individual students, and most importantly, the differences as learners that are likely to be as varied among this category of student as those in any other category or none. Thus, by inhibiting thinking in this direction, the category encourages a focus on the perceived differ-ence which in this instance is behaviour rather than learning.

Whilst the experience of young people in other categories that we may currently consider require additional support for learning may have had similar experiences, the case of learners who may be experiencing social, emotional or behavioural difficulties is more pointed. There can be some sympathy for other groups of disadvantaged learners and, in addition, they or their supporters are able to articulate the arguments that allow them to question the status quo. Matthews (2006) argues that this is a vital part of the process which he terms deliberative democracy, in which members of communities are able to discuss and debate the different points of view and opinion held among the members of that community as part of its process of problem solving and development. In the case of young people who may be experiencing social, emotional or behavioural difficulties, however, they are seen as the problem and, whilst in most cases allowed some form of voice in relation to their behaviour, are often denied the opportunity to contribute to the debate as learners in the same way that other pupils would be.

This is a complex context that comprises the identities of both learners and teachers. Children can be acutely aware of this complex mix of identity and how they interact to determine difference:

> Many children have an intuitive feel for these complexities. They state that one of the main attributes they want from teachers is 'fair-ness' – that is, being treated the same. At the same time, they want to be valued for who they are. (Matthews, 2006, p. 27)

Thus, in the milieu of the classroom, the interactions between teachers and pupils can be seen as a continual process of identity creation: both personal and group identities, and both pupil and teacher identities. Thus, pupil identity and the SEBD category are social constructs to which all parties contribute.

By implication, if not actually, the experience of the classroom for both learners and teachers is an emotional one, and one's emotional disposition is as important as the theory of behaviour to which one subscribes in the creation of the identities both of learners who may be experiencing social, emotional or behavioural difficulties and of their teachers.

Emotional development helps people interact with and recognise others whom they consider to be 'other' than themselves. Equally, lack of emotional development serves to reinforce negative perceptions and to constrain the interactions between teachers and pupils, thereby inhibiting the continuing changing and construction of new identities.

There can be no question that the experience of learning in the classroom involves a high degree of emotional labour for both teachers and pupils. Teachers, as the adults in the classroom, are continually under pressure to control their emotions. Matthews (2006) argues that this was always the case but that in more recent times the pressure to get exam results and the consequent need to teach to a curriculum and timetable for national exams has increased levels of stress for teachers. This, he argues, compares unfavourably with past regimes where the emphasis was on understanding and where progress was seen as greater depth rather than performance in tests and examinations. At the same time, the current regime results in reduced opportunities for teachers to interact with their students in ways that help explore the young people's beliefs and opinions, to compare them with others, and to help develop the maturity that is part of the education of the whole person.

The teacher's task, as it is currently constituted, demands that teachers concentrate on performance goals rather than learning outcomes (Dweck, 2000), thereby suppressing children's needs for creativity, expression and to learn in a myriad of ways that often stray from linear learning but lead to exciting and exhilarating learning that is meaningful to the child. If this is contrary to the teacher's beliefs about children and how they learn, the emotional labour involved increases. The demands of the curriculum to be taught in this way, coupled with workload and the pressure for good exam results, have led to increased teacher stress. It is little surprise, therefore, that when confronted with the type of behaviour that challenges linear teaching and for which there is no time for discussion, that teachers' and schools' natural reaction is to revert to behaviourist approaches of punishment and reward.

Equally, of course, participation in this form of education involves emotional labour for pupils, and again it is no surprise that when emotional or behavioural needs are not being met except by a response based on rewards and sanctions rather than understanding and empowerment, that they, in turn, react in challenging ways.

Moreover, such interaction serves to reinforce what Dweck (2000) calls entity theories of intelligence and personality. Entity theorists believe that intelligence is fixed, usually as a result of biological or genetic factors, and cannot be developed or increased except, perhaps, minimally. Incrementalists, on the other hand, hold the belief that intelligence is dynamic and can grow and that a range of factors (including the environment) have an impact on how it is developed. Similarly with personality, entity theorists hold the belief that people have fixed traits that are inherent parts of their make up and that cannot change. Incrementalists, of course, hold the opposite view. These opposing sets of assumptions are important to both teachers and pupils in the construction and maintenance of their own and others' identities.

Assigning pupils to the SEBD category tends to reinforce entity theories. It suggests certain fixed pupil dispositions (as discussed above) that and removal into a 'special' context such as a behaviour support base helps to fix these traits in the minds of both learners and teachers. The more teachers are encouraged to think this way, the more they are likely to see exclusion of young people whose behaviour they find difficult as the natural and only solution, even although on a personal basis their preferred approaches would be best understood by humanist, incrementalist theories. Similarly, labelling, exclusion and assignment to segregated provision serve to reinforce pupils' entity views of themselves, thus rendering them vulnerable, powerless, and with a possibly negative impact on their self-esteem. Overall, the prognosis is generally pessimistic for both teachers and learners.

Incrementalists, on the other hand, recognise that not all young people who might be experiencing social, emotional or behavioural difficulties are the same or that they even belong to a homogenous group. Instead, they hold the belief that young people can and will change in response to their actions as teachers, and their explanations of young people's behaviour is such that they can envisage the possibility of change.

What then, are the implications of the various beliefs held by teachers and pupils for teaching and learning? It is probable that behaviourists will have a pessimistic view of young people with behavioural difficulties as learners and everything they do is likely to focus on minimising the impact of the behaviour. Since they are also liable to hold behaviourist theories of learning (indeed, as is argued above, are reinforced in this belief by the pressures of the education system), then learning will be presumed to be minimal with low performance goals being the subject of targets for both behaviour and learning.

Teachers whose classroom practice can be understood and explained by humanist values are more usually disposed towards an optimistic view of the learners with whom they work. Their focus is more likely to be on learning rather than behaviour and they are more inclined to use teaching methods that have learning as their prime purpose. They are more of a mind to see the similarities among learners, whilst acknowledging and valuing their individuality. Thus they are liable to subscribe to more social theories of learning and to encourage children and young people to learn together, and to develop pedagogies that are challenging, interactive and transformative.

The reality, of course, is never as simple. Teachers whose 'normal' classroom behaviour can be explained in terms of humanist/incremental theories may choose to deal with learning and behaviour in behaviourist ways in certain circumstances, for example, taking control for young people who may be out of control. Teachers are, above all, practitioners and as such will shift among elements of practice that can be explained and understood by each of the theories discussed in this chapter. The experience of their pupils, and the teachers' own perception, comprehension and appreciation of the classroom will depend upon the emphasis. Regardless of what teachers choose to do in their classrooms, it is vital that they are clear why they are doing what they are doing and fully understand the implications of their actions for the learning, behaviour and development of themselves and the young people whom they teach.

Chapter 3

THE LEGISLATION AND POLICY CONTEXT

As in all other areas of education, provision and practice for young people who might be experiencing social, emotional or behavioural difficulties is guided by policy and legislation. Throughout the 1990s and into the twenty-first century, there has been a raft of policy initiatives that have been significant for the educational experience of young learners whom schools have found difficult to teach. As indicated in previous chapters, much of this movement was itself guided by the international rights agenda, particularly that of UNESCO. The impact of the United Nations materials in Scotland has been to urge the Scottish Office, and subsequently the Scottish Executive, to seek similar practice and provision for all pupils whilst addressing what are perceived to be the different needs of young people experiencing social, emotional or behavioural difficulties.

What is policy?
Policies and guidelines are statements issued by authoritative bodies, usually, in the case of education, local or national governments. Ultimately, the purpose of these policies is to guide teachers and schools in how they go about their work with young learners. Policies reflect the intentions of governments and the interested parties (or at least those powerful enough to have a voice) from whom they seek advice or whose views they take into consideration. Policies, therefore, are political in nature both in general and party terms.

Even from the earliest times, there has been recognition in policy that, even where special education was segregated, that there should nevertheless be a close relationship between special and mainstream schools (Riddell, 2006, p. 5). By the mid twentieth century, there were nine recognised categories of 'handicap' for which special provision could be made, one of which was 'maladjustment', the forerunner of 'social, emotional and behavioural difficulties'. The use of the terms 'maladjustment' and 'SEBD' reflect the different thinking within policies. The former readily points towards individual pupil deficit in that they have failed to or have not fully adapted to the norms of society, or the norms of mainstream education. As described in Chapter 2, deficit was confirmed through a process of ascertainment, including medical examination. The current term, however, represents a shift in focus from the individual's pathological disposition in the direction of cause and recognition that a young person's behaviour in school is dependent upon their experience of life, including life beyond school. Whilst there is no longer a requirement for medical diagnosis, educational psychologists would normally have some input into the support of young people who might be experiencing social, emotional, or behavioural difficulties.

The impetus for this shift in thinking, and crucial for the development of educational policy in Scotland, were the HMI (SED, 1978) and Warnock (DES, 1978) reports. Although there had long been arguments that recognised the relationship between what was being offered in schools, how it was taught and students' behaviour, Warnock and HMI were landmark policies in that they shifted the emphasis from children's difficulties to the school environment, with suggestions that changes in the way that schools were organised and how teachers taught would be likely to lead to more young people experiencing more of their education in mainstream settings.

Warnock questioned the viability of the nine categories of handicap and instead suggested a continuum of SEN. Where a child 'belonged' on this continuum was dependent upon the severity of their difficulty, rather than any specified pathological deficiency. In Scotland this led to the introduction of the Record of Needs incorporated into the Education (Scotland) Act 1980.

The HMI progress report, *The Education of Pupils with Learning Difficulties in Primary and Secondary Schools in Scotland* (SED, 1978), was much more radical in its questioning of permanent segregated provision, deficit laden 'remedial' approaches, and in its advocacy of a pedagogical solution to the teaching and learning of young people who may be experiencing difficulties with their learning. The report advised that, whilst the learning aims for all young people should be the same, they need not be learning the same things at the same time or in the same way. Moreover, the report advocated contextualised rather than de-contextualised learning, and that learning should be enjoyable, creative and allow for the experience of success (Riddell, 2006).

The report also championed a move away from didactic, whole-class teaching and traditional learning towards more interactive methodologies including discussion and group work. In redefining the role of the remedial teacher to include consultancy for colleagues and school managers, the report recognised that learning difficulties, including manifestations of 'inappropriate' behaviour, could be affected by the classroom context and that teachers, as well as pupils, might benefit from support. Among the list of possible roles and tasks indicated for the learning support teacher was the provision of a 'haven for pupils with "temporary emotional upsets"' (Riddell, 2006, p. 9).

It would appear, therefore, that the tension between the desire to provide specialist education whilst at the same time including as many pupils as possible in mainstream schools, was never more observable in the ambiguity in policy and its consequent provision for young people who may be experiencing social, emotional or behavioural difficulties. Whilst 'maladjusted' children had been recognised as one of the nine categories of handicap, and whilst the HMI report recognised the need to cater for such learners, they were not included in the range of learners who could obtain a Record of Needs and were therefore denied access to the resources the Record could attract and the legal strength it held. It could be argued, therefore, that policy resulted in the marginalisation of this group of young people, even if by default rather than intention.

With the establishment of the Scottish Parliament in 1999, the Labour government's policy of social inclusion led to an accelerated movement towards inclusion in education. However, whilst the Standards in Scotland's Schools etc. (Scotland) Act 2000 introduced the presumption of mainstreaming for all pupils, and indicated that segregated education should be the exception, it nevertheless offered three sets of circumstances that would allow local authorities to educate some pupils elsewhere other than mainstream. Apart from unreasonable cost and unsuitability to the pupil's ability and aptitude, the Act allowed for the segregated education of some young people if their inclusion in mainstream would not be compatible with the provision of efficient education for other children. Clearly, this last circumstance refers to young people with whose behaviour schools find it difficult to cope.

However, whilst children and young people who may be experiencing social, emotional or behavioural difficulties may have been marginalised, they were never abandoned. The Scottish Executive's pursuit of inclusion led to the extension of the list of young people requiring additional support to include, among others, young people experiencing social, emotional and behavioural difficulties. As a result, the group of young people categorised as having SEBD gained the same 'legal' force as other young people with learning difficulties and, like them, became entitled to a Coordinated Support Plan, introduced to replace the Record of Needs.

Most notably, the Education (Additional Support for Learning) (Scotland) Act 2004 enshrined the term 'additional support needs' in law, replacing 'SEN' as the preferred term. This new term is perceived to be more inclusive of all learners and has been broadly welcomed. The Record of Needs was to be phased out and replaced by Coordinated Support Plans. These are now being opened for all young people who require regular contact with services beyond the schools and education authorities. The shift in language represents the shift in Scottish Executive thinking on inclusion away from pupil deficit towards provision. However, whilst the Act and its accompanying code of practice, *Supporting Children's Learning*

(SEED, 2005) give examples of what schools might do to support a range of pupils, there is nevertheless more than a trace of deficit thinking in the measures suggested for dealing with young people's behaviour (see below). This is not least apparent in the new term 'additional support needs' itself. Whilst there is acknowledgement that all children will require support for their learning at some time (SEED, 2005), the use of the term 'additional' suggests that for the groups of children and young people involved, this is over and above what might otherwise be considered normal. Moreover, by focusing on needs, the Act and code imply the approach of Warnock and HMI by reinforcing the needs agenda at the expense of the rights agenda that has emerged since the mid-1990s.

Arising from the legislation and in support of policy, a number of guidelines were produced throughout the 1990s and into the new century, aimed at supporting the learning of school pupils who might be experiencing difficulties with their behaviour. The documents examined below are not all of the documents produced in Scotland that address the issue of providing appropriate curricular experiences for a range of pupils, but they are the principal ones which have affected teaching and learning within the context of SEBD. They represent the major influences on what happens in classes in order to support pupils in developing both cognitive and affective elements in the pursuit of a holistic educational experience.

Support for Learning 5–14 *(SfL 5–14)*

The 5–14 framework for pupils with SEBD (SCCC, 1994) was based on the five principles of breadth, balance, continuity, coherence and progression. Throughout this document there is an emphasis on flexibility in approach in order to ensure that, for the pupil with SEBD, there is an 'appropriate balance between formal academic work and personal and social development' (SCCC, 1994, p. 9). In particular, it is suggested that an emphasis on language and number should be avoided.

Similarly, in constructing programmes of study, the document advised the use of the five key strategies of differentiation, individualisation, adaptation, enhancement and elaboration. Again, this part of the document was concerned with the practicalities of providing an appropriate curriculum and the need for schools to be flexible and creative in their approach. There was also advice that students themselves should be involved in the planning of their own curriculum, a practice that has become increasingly prevalent in schools, particularly through the operation of Individualised Educational Programmes, Personal Development Plans and suchlike.

A Manual of Good Practice *(MGP)*

MGP (SOEID, 1999) section 2B dealt with Providing an Appropriate Curriculum. Subsection 2B1 dealt with Learning and Teaching and subsection

2B2 looked at Planning the Curriculum. Much of the detail of what was said in MGP is similar to that found in SfL 5–14, but the tone and emphasis could be seen as somewhat different. For example, whilst MGP also advocated personal and social development, there was a stronger emphasis on target setting in language and number in both mainstream and special settings. Moreover, within MGP whilst the principles and strategies in SfL 5–14 were acknowledged, there was a clear emphasis on individualisation, with the Individualised Educational Programme (and target setting within it) being the main instrument of curricular development. This can be clearly seen in the statement adopted from *Effective Provision for Special Educational Needs* (EPSEN) (SOED, 1994):

> Appropriate education for children and young persons with special educational needs is that which assists them to make the fullest use of their potential for learning and comprises three essential components a well thought-out curriculum for the class/school as a whole, individualised educational programmes, and integration of the IEPs with the curriculum for the class/school. (EPSEN 1.8 in SOEID, 1999, p. 44)

The overall argument of MGP was that a progressive and appropriate curriculum, based on entitlement and equal opportunity was the right of children with special needs. This curriculum should provide a quality educational experience for students, and parents should be involved in the development of that experience.

The Heart of the Matter *(HoM)*

HoM (SCCC, 1995) was founded on five qualities or dispositions. These were respect and caring for self; respect and caring for others; a sense of social responsibility; a commitment to learning; and a sense of belonging. In order to achieve these, HoM suggested there should be a focus on four essential skills, namely personal and interpersonal skills; communication skills; the ability to engage with problems; and learning skills. The overall purpose of a curriculum based on these qualities and skills was expressed as enabling learners to function effectively as individuals and as learners; to form considerate and supportive relationships; to interact effectively with the natural and social environment; to make the transition to adult and working life; and to operate effectively within the community.

Much of what was contained in HoM could be said to be what teachers would intuit. It pointed to the importance of feeling, both in terms of educational achievements and, going beyond school, 'a personally rewarding life, productive employment and effective citizenship' (SCCC, 1995, p. 1). Again, however, there were important social issues that impinged on pupils, teachers and families and influenced their attitudes towards what they considered to be an appropriate curriculum. One could question, for instance, if employment was (and still is) a realistic hope for many pupils, or even whether that is a legitimate purpose of a curriculum for anyone. Likewise the notion of citizenship may be difficult to encompass for those who feel excluded.

Notwithstanding the difficulties and contradictions among documents emanating from ostensibly the same source, at the centre of each of the guidelines there is recognition of the importance of personal and social development (PSD). The thinking behind PSD lies in the recognition that feelings and thinking are equally important factors in learning. If people feel good about themselves they will thrive and, therefore, learn. Conversely, if they do not value themselves, are not motivated or see no point in their subject of study, they will not learn. The close link between the cognitive and affective domains of the human psyche has been closely studied in recent years. In particular, Howard Gardner's (1993) work on intra- and inter-personal skills and Daniel Goleman's (1996) writing on emotional intelligence have been influential in rethinking approaches to learning. At a very basic, but highly practical, level we have all experienced distressed, disaffected and worried children who, because of their emotional state, are not predisposed to learn. Indeed, we as adults would not be inclined to learn if we were preoccupied with difficult matters.

However, at least in part because PSD is a relatively new area for teachers who are used to a subject or topic-based curriculum, there appears to be little or no agreement as to what actually constitutes PSD. Moreover, the subject itself would appear to have low status within many (perhaps, especially secondary) schools in west-central Scotland. No teacher has a degree or subject specialism in PSD, those who teach it in schools are known not as PSD teachers but as subject or class teachers who take PSD classes, and, consequently, students see it as 'not a real subject'. Many teachers, including those who see genuine benefit in PSD, consider themselves to be less knowledgeable in PSD than in their subjects, are not given the time or the materials to prepare as meticulously for PSD in comparison to their curricular areas, and, as a result feel themselves to be less effective in their delivery of PSD. It may be the case that this situation has worsened in recent years as pastoral care has become part of the remit of all teachers. Children perceive this and, taking their lead from the school, treat the subject less seriously. Perhaps this can be illustrated through an example from practice (Case study 3).

Case study 3

In a secondary behaviour support base, there was a strong emphasis on PSD in the pupils' work. However, staff noted that, in comparison to other activities that took place, the students did not take this seriously. Additionally, they compared PSD unfavourably with more traditional subject areas. When asked why, they said it was because it was not a real subject. They explained that both at the base and in their mainstream schools, all that happened in PSD was that they were given a work sheet, they filled it out and there was some teacher-directed discussion. This may or may not have been all that was happening. Indeed, our own experiences should indicate that in some cases at least, much more was going on. However, what was important here was the children's perception of what was happening. So staff asked them what the difference was between PSD and a real subject. The pupils informed the teachers that, in a real subject, students have a jotter, the teacher tells them things and they write them in their jotters. Pupils are then given questions or exercises and these, again, are done in their jotters. At the end of term an exam is set in the subject. Following their advice, staff gave what they were doing a name (*Self-Science* after Daniel Goleman) and announced it as a new subject. They issued jotters and indicated that there would be tests at various stages and an exam at the end of term. The use of worksheets was cut to a minimum and the delivery of the curriculum was styled more along traditional lines as they were described by the children. As you may guess, the effect was immediate.

In the above example, the content of the programme, whilst remaining basically the same, developed in response to what the pupils told staff. Thus, whilst previously teachers might have offered anger management, this was now included in a section of the self-science curriculum in which the class looked at how the body functions at times of stress (for example what happens to your breathing) what is happening within the brain which causes this, and things that can be done to alter what is happening. The children accepted and engaged with this 'scientific' study rather than being provided with a fix for their problems. Thus young people in this instance were able to discern as patronising the presentation of aspects of behaviour support that suggested deficit. At the same time, they were able to appreciate that learning about emotions and their physical effect on the self was valuable. This may have been because the focus was on the topic that generated insight into and understanding of the pupils' own experiences without in any way suggesting that their individual behaviour was other than 'normal' in the circumstances. Crucially, the approach taken by behaviour support teachers in this case was posited on the belief that the development of knowledge and insight, rather than the imposition of social norms, is critical for the formation of attitudes and habits that will enable young people to deal with life in school and beyond.

By way of contrast to the case study example above, practice in the area of SEN has increasingly been seen as overly bureaucratic and outdated. *Assessing Our Children's Needs: The Way Forward?* was published in 2002. The document engaged in consultation and many teachers, headteachers and other educationalists contributed their views to this process. The need for a more up-to-date system expressed in the document has seen the arrival of the Education (Additional Support for Learning) (Scotland) Act 2004. This Act seeks to drive forward the move for inclusion and seeks to update and enhance much of the good practice in existence. This new Act is the first major revision of SEN legislation since the Education (Scotland) Act 1980.

Better Behaviour – Better Learning: Report of the Discipline Task Group

In response to teachers' earlier concerns about a perceived increase in indiscipline in schools, the then Education Minister, Jack McConnell, set up the Discipline Task Group (DTG). Following consultation with a wide range of stakeholders and interested parties, the DTG issued their report, *Better Behaviour – Better Learning* in June 2001. From the outset, the report established a focus on 'the inescapable links between good discipline and effective learning and teaching' (SEED, 2001, p. 7).

Moreover, recent initiatives in Scottish education such as *Assessing our Children's Needs: The Way Forward?* (SEED, 2002), *Moving Forward: Additional Support for Learning* (SEED, 2003) and the Education (Additional Support for Learning) (Scotland) Act 2004 imply a shift in focus from viewing the requirement of additional support for some pupils as a matter of disability and pupil deficit towards one of ability and students' learning. Within this general context, there has been a move towards recognising social, emotional and behavioural difficulties as a learning difficulty. The recommendations in SEED (2001) are that pupils requiring additional support on the grounds of SEBD might be offered the same systems of support as any other young person requiring additional support for learning: 'pupils experiencing social, emotional and behavioural difficulties . . . clearly have special educational needs, and as such, should receive support strategies similar to those commonly employed for learning difficulties' (SEED, 2001, p. 13).

This places SEBD within the context of social justice and the rights agenda, and *Better Behaviour – Better Learning* indicates this in its recommendations for the empowerment of students and teachers:

> All members of the school community are of equal worth and are entitled to respect. There is no place for discrimination based on race, ethnic origin, religion, gender, sexual orientation, disability, social group or any other grounds. Schools must ensure equality of opportunity and access to education for all children and young people with particular regard being paid to those learners with disabilities and special needs. (SEED, 2001, p. 8)

These documents recognise that dealing with additional support needs and SEBD, in particular in classes, is a complex and difficult business and one that should not necessarily be left to teachers alone. The nature of some of these difficulties is given a degree of prominence in *Better Behaviour – Better Learning*, especially the need to work with pupils, parents and other adults and professionals in a holistic approach to supporting young people with SEBD. Once more, however, the areas given less coverage are the specific nature of the pupil behaviour the policy makers would like to see developed in place of 'inappropriate' behaviour, and equally important, the teacher practice required to achieve this.

The relationship between learning, teaching and behaviour is given prominence in several sections of the early part of the DTG report and the nature of that relationship can be gleaned from the discourse used:

> Effective learning and teaching is much easier to achieve where a positive ethos and good discipline prevail. Discipline policy cannot, and should not, be separated from policy on learning and teaching – the two are inextricably linked. Children and young people are more likely to engage positively with education when careful consideration is given to the factors which affect their learning and teaching.(SEED, 2001, p. 8)

This paragraph reveals the thinking behind the report. The bulk of it recognises that, for teachers, regardless of how they deal with students' behaviour, it has to be seen in a context of their learning.

However, the first sentence of the above paragraph indicates a particular approach to dealing with the learning of young people with SEBD that may be quite different from that used to deal with the learning of other young people. The thrust of this first sentence can be understood to indicate that the establishment of a 'positive ethos and good discipline' is a prerequisite condition for 'effective learning and teaching'. Indeed, this thinking can also be seen in the title of the report where the word order indicates that in order for learning to take place, behaviour has first of all to be addressed. This is essentially different to how teachers would approach the learning of other pupils with learning difficulties. Most obviously, teachers would not attempt to 'fix' the sight or hearing of a pupil with a visual or hearing impairment; rather they would start by asking, 'How do I address the learning of this student?'

Furthermore, the report suggests that pupil behaviour be dealt with through a process of 'positive discipline' and 'positive behaviour', terms that appear to be used synonymously throughout the document. These terms are redolent of the work of Canter and Canter (1992) in America. Indeed, recommendation 6 makes this connection clear where it states that 'Particular attention should be paid to expectation, rules, rewards and sanctions' (SEED, 2001, p. 2). Moreover, the report goes on to delineate the approach (sections 2.21, 2.22 and 2.23) in terms of rules, rewards and sanctions that echo a behaviourist approach to dealing with young people who have attracted the SEBD label (Garner and Gains, 1996). Indeed, it is noticeable here that none of the seventeen statements that describe rules, rewards and sanctions contains an explicit reference to learning. The behaviourist, positive behaviour and discipline approach has long been criticised as being contrary to the rights agenda and, indeed, reinforcing the kind of behaviour that it sets out to eliminate (Kohn, 1996; Watkins and Wagner, 2000). In schools this argument is complicated by the fact, recognised in the report, that 'there is no agreement on what counts as a social, emotional or behavioural difficulty' (SEED, 2001, p. 13).

Therefore, there are two difficulties with the approach suggested by the DTG. Firstly, the recommendation of positive discipline may, in fact, operate against the achievement of other recommendations concerning pupil and teacher empowerment. Secondly, once again, there is no clear or agreed idea of the behaviour that to be eliminated or, more significantly, the behaviour with which it is to be replaced. Furthermore, it could be argued that analysing and addressing children's behaviour is more properly the domain of psychology and social work. The report itself does recognise this in its sections on working with parents, supporting pupils in schools and multidisciplinary working. That is not to say that teachers can abrogate their responsibilities in this area and indeed, it has been shown that whilst not therapists, nevertheless teachers' actions in class can have a highly therapeutic effect for students (Munn *et al.*, 2000). The answer may be to do as the report itself recommends: to treat SEBD like any other learning difficulty. The priority for the teacher then becomes the child's learning. The report recognises this when discussing the need for local solutions to the problems that arise: 'It is clear that "solutions" to indiscipline cannot be grafted from elsewhere onto a school's own context and culture' (SEED, 2001, p. 7).

The discussion at this point in the document may well have been about physical locations, the 'where' of additional support, but the same argument could apply to professional domains or the 'how' of additional support for learning. Whilst it is right and proper that the disciplines of psychology and social work inform what teachers do, they cannot take priority over or replace the teacher's prime function: to deal with the learning of all young people. The 'culture and context' of schools is teaching and learning and these are the expectations that teachers and students have of school. Where these expectations are shared and agreed, it is possible to develop a sense of community based on them. In dealing with behaviour, the concept of community is important because:

community is aimed not just at improving student behavior but at creating the kinds of ties that bond students together and students and teachers together and that bind them to shared ideas and ideals. (Sergiovanni, 1994, p. 120)

It appears obvious that the 'ties that bond' and the 'shared ideas' will have to do with teaching and learning, and the suggestion is that where these are the basis of the relationship between teacher and pupil there is an improvement in behaviour. In addition, recent research has shown that there is a 'need for a wider discussion of the curriculum and pedagogy of schools' (Lloyd *et al.*, 2003, p. 89) in supporting children who may be experiencing SEBD. Furthermore, schools that consider themselves successful in supporting young people, 'were committed to keeping pupils "on track" and engaged in learning' (Turner and Waterhouse, 2003, p. 25).

The DTG is again aware of the efficacy of this approach in eliminating some behavioural difficulties:

It seems clear that where appropriate consideration is given to learning and teaching approaches and where the quality of learning and teaching is consistently high, with the appropriate balance of challenge and support enshrined within an atmosphere of high expectation, discipline problems can be reduced significantly. (SEED, 2001, p. 18)

In order to do this, the starting point has to be pupils' learning and not their behaviour. Beginning with students' learning also suggests the kind of behaviour that is most appropriate for our students, namely, learning behaviour. However, the concept of 'learning behaviour' and the process of how we go about developing it require some illumination, which will be the subject matter of the following chapters.

Supporting Children's Learning: Code of Practice

In 2005, following much consultation and a draft code, the Scottish Executive published their code of practice for dealing with the learning of all young people with additional support needs in the context of inclusion. *Supporting Children's Learning* places the education of all young people requiring additional support for learning firmly within the rights agenda and details a list of parents' and young people's rights in the process of establishing whether or not a child requires additional support, the provision that will be made, and how they can contribute to and contest decisions made concerning a Coordinated Support Plan and provision (SEED, 2005, p. 14). Indeed, in their introduction to the code, the ministers highlight this point:

It gives [parents] more say in their child's education and more opportunities to express their views about what support they feel their
child needs. It helps them in their dealings with the local authority if
they feel that their child is not getting the support which they think
is required. And it provides children and young people themselves
with opportunities to have their views considered in those significant
decisions that affect their education. (p. 1)

The focus, however, is still clearly on needs. Whilst the term 'special
education' has been replaced by 'additional support', 'additional support
needs' are still defined in deficit terms:

A child or young person has additional support needs . . . where,
for whatever reason, the child or young person is, or is likely to be,
unable without the provision of additional support to benefit from
school education . . . (p. 15)

Additional support itself is defined as

provision which is additional to, or otherwise different from, the
educational provision made generally for children or, as the case
may be, young persons of the same age in schools (other than special
schools) under the management of the education authority for the
area to which the child or young person belongs. (p. 15)

Whilst the Act and code of practice, therefore, might well be more optimistic than previous documents, especially for children and young people who
may be experiencing SEBD, they nevertheless render inclusion as, at best, a
work-in-progress and an aspiration rather than an educational requirement.

The focus on needs has two detrimental effects. Firstly, it deflects from
the issue of rights thereby allowing the rights of one group to be set against
the rights of others. Quite simply, if all pupils have the right to learn alongside their peers, then that right is inalienable. However, as often happens
when a student's behaviour becomes difficult, their right to learn is set
against the right of the others in the class not to have their learning disrupted
and it is argued that the pupil who is misbehaving has forfeited his or her
right to be in the class or even school.

Secondly, whilst the code introduces a shift away from solely pupil
deficit towards recognition that appropriate provision is important, it is nevertheless provision aimed at particular groups. Adopting this stance implies
that the educational needs of these groups of students is different from other
peer groups. This is highly questionable and it is argued elsewhere (Head,
2005) that the educational needs of all children are, in fact, the same: it is
the nature and extent of the support required to meet pupils' rights to be
educated alongside their peers that varies. Since the code and Act them-

selves recognise that all children will at some time require support for their learning, then support itself should not be seen as 'additional' but simply varied from student to student and from time to time.

These arguments apart, however, the code does offer a note of optimism for young people whose behaviour is problematic for schools. Significantly, the list of reasons cited for the source of children's and young people's additional support needs includes the following, each of which are features commonly pertaining to young people who receive behaviour support:

- are being bullied;
- are looked after;
- are living with parents who are abusing substances;
- are living with parents who have mental health problems;
- are not attending school regularly;
- have emotional or social difficulties;
- are on the child protection register. (SEED, 2005, p. 11)

Naturally, not all children who may have one or more of the above as aspects of their lives will present behaviour that is difficult for schools to deal with, but it tends to be the case that most of the young people who receive behaviour support of some kind have at least one of these features as part of their profile. The importance of the inclusion of these reasons, however, is that children and young people who might be experiencing difficulties as a result of them may now be considered to have additional support needs in the same way as any other young person with physical, sensory, or learning difficulties and could be entitled to a Coordinated Support Plan. Thus, the concept of behavioural difficulties as a learning difficulty as established in the DTG report (SEED, 2001) is reinforced.

The code recognises that whilst there is 'a wide range of factors which may lead to children and young people having a need for additional support' (SEED, 2005, p. 19) they nevertheless fall into four broad categories of the learning environment, family circumstances, disability or health need, and social and emotional factors. Within the learning environment, the code recognises the importance of the school ethos and appropriate approaches to learning and teaching, the subject matter of the final chapter of this book. The family circumstances described as contributing towards a requirement for additional support include those listed above, some of which are typical of young people receiving behaviour support. Within the disability and health category, the code suggests that autistic spectrum disorder and attention deficit hyperactivity disorder can be contributory factors towards a requirement for additional support. Again, many of the young people and children receiving behaviour support are often somewhere on the autistic spectrum (though probably not diagnosed) or have or display the signs of attention deficit disorder or attention deficit hyperactivity disorder. Contributory factors in the social and emotional category include bullying (both victims and perpetrators), racial discrimination and offending in the community.

The grouping together of these factors represents a significant development in policy regarding the educational experience of young people whose additional support provision includes some form of behaviour support. In addition to conceptualising behavioural difficulties as a learning difficulty, the recognition that none of these categories is discrete, and in particular recognition of the impact of the learning environment on learning, are highly significant for schools and teachers. Teachers, support assistants and others primarily responsible for the education of young people may have some limited level of impact on family, the community and health issues but they can have major impact on the learning environment. This aspect of policy with its implication of freedom and flexibility to the classroom teacher and the school as a whole resounds with hope for our schools, teachers and all young people. Indeed, the desire within the code to move away from individual pupil deficit as the focus for decisions on additional support is made explicit in the section in which they argue that a need for additional support does not imply lack of ability, skills or talent. One example given being: 'A young person with social and emotional difficulties may have talents in one area of learning or be capable of attaining highly across the curriculum' (SEED, 2005, p. 20).

Thus, in this latest policy document, children and young people who may be experiencing SEBD have ceased to be demonised in ways that they have been in the past. However, whilst there is optimism in the example given above, some might still see such statements as patronising and the recognition that 'different' (read 'segregated') provision is still an option, will, it could be argued, still result in the marginalisation of young people receiving behaviour support.

Why is this the case?

Riddell (2006) argues that the dominant model of administering social justice and inclusion in Scotland has been bureaucratic professionalism. The main features of this model are a system of agreed procedures in order to provide an appropriate service to meet individual needs. However, the procedures tend to be those developed by the administration at either local or national level, and the provision is that currently available within a local authority. The main consequence of operating this model has been that inclusion in Scotland's schools has been dominated by the views of local authorities, schools and teachers. Even within what Riddell describes as a move towards a more consumerist model, the consumer voice encouraged is that of the parent and not the pupil. Indeed, some might argue that, certainly within the field of SEBD, only the voices of the most vociferous parents are heard at all, and that bureaucratic professionalism remains the operational model. As a result, notions of choice for children and young people who might be experiencing SEBD are spurious, where they exist at all.

Another possible reason for the continued marginalisation of this group of learners lies in the fact that whilst policies at national and local levels reflect a commitment to inclusion, there is no clear definition of what it means. In addition, national policy has left local authorities free to develop and operate inclusion in whichever way they see as most appropriate for their context. Consequently, in addition to the diverse range of provision in different authorities ranging from no segregation to the maintenance of special schools described in Chapter 1, the educational experience of any learner with additional support needs depends on how policy operates within the local authority in which they live.

A third possible contributing factor, especially to the exclusionist experience of learners who might be experiencing SEBD is the thrust of some educational policies that have been perceived to conflict with inclusion policies. In particular, polices aimed at raising attainment are seen as being in opposition to inclusion.

It would appear, therefore, that within the policy context, as with the theory and research contexts, there are dichotomies that may serve to reinforce the historical, segregationist approaches that patronise, demonise and marginalise the learning of vulnerable children and young people. One possible approach to overcoming these perceived dichotomies is to look at what each of the policies has in common and shift the focus of thinking in that direction. The shared concern, naturally, is teaching and learning and it is the teaching and learning of pupils who may be experiencing SEBD that is the subject of the next chapter.

Chapter 4

RESEARCH

This chapter examines recent research into the educational experiences of young people who may be experiencing SEBD, and those of their teachers. The materials used are, principally, research carried out by staff at the Faculty of Education in the University of Glasgow (Head *et al.*, 2002), research commissioned by the Scottish Executive and carried out by researchers from the University of Edinburgh (Munn *et al.*, 2004) and by National Foundation for Educational Research (Wilkin *et al.*, 2006). Thereafter, consideration will be given to how research involving young people who might be experiencing SEBD might develop.

Between June 2000 and December 2001 a team from the University of Glasgow evaluated the effectiveness of behaviour support in one Scottish local authority's secondary schools. The context was the Scottish Executive's incentive to local authorities to develop more inclusive approaches to the education of young people who might be experiencing SEBD. The local authority involved in this study enabled each of its secondary schools to shape its own response to the initiative, resulting in the emergence of sometimes very different forms of behaviour support across schools. The evaluation project set out to answer four questions: what was working; where were systems not working; what else was needed; and was the initiative providing value for money? The last of these questions proved unanswerable from the available data.

The Scottish Executive initiative, *Alternative to Exclusion*, was basically a target setting initiative, specifically, to reduce exclusions from school by one third over a period of two years. Target setting approaches have been criticised as leading to superficial and short-term approaches to the problem of exclusions (Cooper *et al.*, 2000; Munn *et al.*, 2000; Parsons, 1999). Indeed, national statistics on exclusions (SEED, 2000) indicate that target setting had no positive impact on exclusion rates across Scotland.

Within the local authority concerned, however, the schools and teachers did achieve a marked reduction in exclusions over the period of the study. What the schools did in order to achieve this can be considered from two perspectives: what took place in schools and classes; and how behaviour support was conceptualised and organised. The following discussion on the approaches utilised in this local authority are based largely on Head *et al.* (2003) and Kane *et al.* (2004).

The range of methods used across schools in the local authority suggested a pragmatic approach to supporting pupils' behaviour. The main elements of practice related to both teachers and pupils. On the one hand support was viewed as something best directed towards individuals experiencing difficulties (for example, through one-to-one support or in small groups), whilst on the other hand it was constructed as support for teachers in the context of the classroom and the curriculum. This latter element anticipated recent initiatives such as staged intervention.

The most frequently used methods of support for young people were those deployed outside the classroom, namely, one-to-one support and small group work (86% in both cases). The work undertaken by behaviour support teachers in these contexts consisted of work related to the curriculum and addressing issues of personal and social development, including counselling and therapeutic approaches such as Solution Focused Therapy. In relation to both types of activity, however, behaviour support teachers expressed reservations concerning their own effectiveness. They highlighted their perceived inability to provide teaching informed by a deep understanding of the core concepts and skills required in curriculum subjects other than their own area of expertise. Similarly, the need for staff development on skills related to a counselling approach was expressed.

Three strategies were employed that did not entail the extraction of pupils from class to a segregated behaviour support base. Rather, these strategies were seen as supporting teachers in addition to young people experiencing difficulties. In order of frequency of deployment, these were: cooperative teaching (71%), target setting and monitoring, and daily behaviour assessment sheets. These latter two were used by less than half of the teachers who participated in the research.

In Scotland, cooperative teaching as a strategy for addressing learning in classes where behaviour is a difficulty, has a pedigree stretching back at least to the HMI Progress Report (SED, 1978), where it was endorsed as one of four 'new' roles for remedial teachers. It is argued (Head *et al.*, 2003) that cooperative teaching has been a major influence on a gradual shift in the way that learning difficulties generally, and behavioural difficulties in particular, have come to be conceptualised. Previously, young people's difficulties in school were seen as a 'within-pupil' deficit. Now, however, it has increasingly come to be recognised that the curriculum and school environment can have a significant impact on young people's learning, including difficulties with behaviour. Environmental factors as an influence on learning and behaviour, and social, emotional and behavioural difficulties as a learning difficulty have become recognised in policy and enshrined in legislation (see Chapter 3).

In addition to being the most frequently used strategy *within* classes (although not utilised to the same extent as extraction) cooperative teaching was seen as the most effective strategy to deal with difficult behaviour (including those measures that involved extraction). Cooperative teaching received the strongest endorsement from respondents with 93% rating it either 'effective' (60%) or 'highly effective' (33%). Moreover, other strategies that did not involve extraction of pupils also attracted high endorsement from teachers, with daily assessment sheets rated 'effective' by 80% and individual target setting rated 'effective' by 67%. However, the two most frequently used methods involved extraction whilst attracting a response of 'effective' by only 47% and 'very effective' by 13% of respondents in each case.

These figures present an interesting picture of behaviour support in this local authority's secondary schools. Although in-class strategies, especially cooperative teaching, were endorsed as more effective, they were used less frequently than strategies involving extraction. This situation can be interpreted as representing a dichotomy between what teachers would prefer to do to support young people and what they actually do or what systems in place in schools allow them to do. There are a number of issues that arise out of this finding, two of which have particular relevance for this book. The first question that needs to be addressed is why teachers prefer to exclude young people from their classes when they report that in-class approaches are more effective. This matter is dealt with in the next chapter. The second issue is that of context. If teachers' actions concerning behaviour in classes reveal a dichotomy between thought and practice, it may be that there are environmental factors informing their views.

Using materials made available as part of the research, it was possible to generate a tripartite typology based on broad distinctions on how behaviour support operated among the schools. A number of studies have highlighted the importance of school ethos or the combined and pervasive influence of relationships, values and attitudes in shaping how schools respond to young people whose behaviour they find challenging (Cooper, 1993; Munn *et al.*, 2000; Visser *et al.*, 2001). Daniels *et al.* (2000), in acknowledging the importance of values, argue that it is the articulation of values in the school setting that is more important than the adoption of a particular set of values. Cooper *et al.* (2000) discuss the interplay between values and structures and argue that schools' success in dealing with young people whom they find difficult is associated with

> the existence of a strong framework of values and a tight relationship between values and structure; and that lesser success might be associated with situations either where there was no strong framework of values shared by the majority of staff, or where the relationship between structures and values was not clearly articulated. (p. 168)

This was, indeed, the case in this study. From data gathered through information provided by schools and indications of schools' values systems, three 'types' of behaviour support emerged.

In some schools, behaviour support was conceptualised as permeating all aspects of provision (this was termed Type 1 support). Support for pupils who may have been experiencing SEBD was set in a context of broader support systems. So, for example, one school developed a study skills programme and targeted it towards particular pupils, including those whose behaviour was problematic. For this type of school, reductions in exclusions were a by-product of approaches designed to address the learning of all young people in the schools. In addition, teachers were encouraged to learn about their own pedagogy and the curriculum was examined closely with the intention of making it more appropriate and inclusive. In these schools, behaviour support could be 'invisible' in that it was not located in a place or a group of people but was embedded in support for pupils' learning. In this type of school, behaviour support was a question of 'how' and not 'where', thus avoiding segregated provision and leading to less marginalisation and possible demonisation of this particular group of young people.

In the second type of school, behaviour support was structured as a discrete entity (Type 2). In these schools, behaviour support was distinct both in terms of having dedicated personnel and in operating approaches to supporting behaviour that were separate from other support systems in the schools. In this model, behaviour support typically involved a few teachers who worked with identified pupils within a specified area or base. Schools operating this type of approach to behaviour support saw a reduction in exclusions as a task to be tackled more directly through the establishment of a base which was, in some cases at least, literally an alternative to exclusion. The role of behaviour support teachers was described by one behaviour support teacher as supporting young people who were excluded to the base and to help them think about their behaviour: '[We give them] a chance to think about it and we can help them by talking about the surface things and help to understand why they have problems in that sort of situation' (Kane *et al.*, 2004, p. 71). In this type of school, then, there was a clear focus on addressing behaviour issues as distinct from learning.

In the third type of school, behaviour support operated as a combination of both the above approaches, with some tending more to one approach than the other (Type 3). In this model, behaviour support was a distinct element in school organisation, usually with identified behaviour support staff. The mode of operation though, tended, to a greater or lesser degree, to be through the ordinary curricular and pastoral systems of the school. The extent to which behaviour support operated within the broader systems or through discrete provision depended on how staff within the school conceptualised the 'problem' and how senior management structured provision.

Sometimes, therefore, behaviour support was linked to learning support departments and mirrored learning support practices such as cooperative teaching. In other schools within this type, behaviour support was structured as distinct from learning support with its own staff and often segregated accommodation. Approaches to behaviour support in these schools were characterised by teachers' and school managers' efforts to strike a balance, encompassing features from the other two models. The majority of schools belonged to this type.

The teachers involved in behaviour support, regardless of the type of school to which they belonged, identified the main purpose of behaviour support as being the reduction of exclusions. However, there were differences in the ways in which this common purpose was pursued. In those schools where behaviour support operated on the permeating model, teachers believed that reductions in exclusions were a helpful side effect of supporting pupils' learning. In some instances, pupils were unaware that they were receiving behaviour support or that behaviour support was in any significant way different from support for learning, generally.

In those schools operating the discrete model, behaviour support could be described as internal exclusion. Bases in these schools operated as 'sin bins' to which pupils were excluded rather than being sent home. Some subject teachers in these schools understood that the purpose of behaviour support was to provide respite for subject teachers and other pupils. Behaviour support teachers, however, saw their purpose also as supporting the individual pupil who was experiencing difficulties. In most cases, some considerable time and attention had been given to developing alternative educational provision for pupils who were in bases. Often this was weighted towards personal and social development. Nevertheless, teachers involved in planning a curriculum for pupils with challenging behaviour recognised that approaches designed primarily to address the affective domain of the mind also had an impact on the cognitive domain, and hence learning. Whilst asserting the value of a focus on personal and social development for their pupils, teachers involved in behaviour support also acknowledged the practical difficulties of offering a full and subject-based curriculum. The principal perceived difficulty was the limited range of subject expertise available from behaviour support staff and their consequent inability to ensure curriculum continuity for pupils coming from or going back into the ordinary mainstream timetable.

In developing behaviour support, schools sought to achieve a balance between apparent polarities – for example between flexibility and structured support; between permeation and visibility; between targeted support and inclusive approaches; and between responsiveness and appropriate prioritising of need. The schools operating the combined model of behaviour support in particular were characterised by their efforts to strike a balance that encompassed all of these features. As the initiative progressed, schools of this type were prepared to try a range of strategies in order to reduce the number of exclusions. Throughout the three years for which data were collected, collaborative strategies, and cooperative teaching in particular, were cited as the preferred methods of support.

In schools of the second and third type, subject teachers expressed concerns regarding the responsiveness of behaviour support staff. They argued that interventions did not happen quickly enough, thereby limiting the capacity of behaviour support to provide respite for teachers, for pupils in difficulty and for other pupils in the class. On the other hand, behaviour support teachers in these same schools complained of being used by subject colleagues solely to contain individual pupils.

By way of a contrast, where staff development took place as a result of interaction between subject and support teachers, different perceptions began to emerge. For example, subject teachers who did some work in a base, even for a short time, developed a deeper appreciation of the difficulties experienced by some of the young people whom they had referred to the base and, consequently, developed a greater empathy with them. Similarly, behaviour support teachers working cooperatively in classrooms with subject teachers gained a clearer understanding of the demands of the curriculum and the strategies needed to manage behaviour in an ordinary class context.

Regardless of the model of behaviour support adopted, all the schools in this study emphasised the increased flexibility that behaviour support offered to the school. However, flexibility could also be interpreted as ambivalence about the purpose and function of behaviour support. In particular, there was a clear division between schools that conceptualised behaviour support as serving a discipline function (e.g. Type 2) and schools that saw it clearly as promoting the welfare of vulnerable pupils (e.g. Type 1).

In 2004, the Scottish Executive published two reports related to children's behaviour in schools. The first of these, *Connect* (SEED, 2004) was a report on the implementation of *Better Behaviour – Better Learning* and amounts to an audit of practice among schools in Scotland's 32 local authorities. The second (Munn *et al.*, 2004) reported on teachers' perceptions of discipline in Scottish schools. The latter report was the third in a series, the previous surveys having been carried out in 1990 and 1996. The report was also used to inform the 2004 policy update discussed in the previous chapter. In 2006, a further report, *Behaviour in Scottish Schools*, based on research carried by a team from the National Foundation for Educational Research (NFER), was published by the Scottish Executive (Wilkin *et al.*, 2006).

Whilst the purpose of *Connect* was to provide an overview of initiatives in each of Scotland's 32 local authorities that could then be shared amongst each other as examples of successful practice, the other two reports sought to examine behaviour in schools in a deeper and more comprehensive manner. The purpose of the two reports can be broadly summarised in the aims of the 2006 document:

> provide evidence on the nature and prevalence of indiscipline;provide evidence on the extent of positive behaviour; examine what is effective in preventing and responding to indiscipline; consider what is effective in promoting positive behaviour.(Wilkin *et al.*, 2006, p. 2)

Whilst the two reports are not strictly comparable in terms of sample size, range and methodology, nevertheless some interesting similarities emerge. Most notably, participants in both surveys agreed that the vast majority of children and young people in Scottish schools were well behaved, that indiscipline tended to be 'low-level' (for example, talking out of turn) and that serious misbehaviour was rare. Most notably, however, both reports stress the highly contextual nature of what constitutes 'bad' or 'inappropriate' behaviour, and, presumably, the consequent experience of children and young people in classes. For example, Munn *et al.* (2004, p. 23) found that male secondary teachers were more likely than their female colleagues to report the discipline situation in their school as serious. Similarly, Wilkin *et al.* (2006, p. 38) reported that those teachers who felt confident in responding to 'indiscipline' were less likely to report (therefore less likely to have perceived) instances of negative behaviour. Moreover, there appeared to be no overall strategy agreed as effective in dealing with children and young people's behaviour (Munn *et al.*, 2004, p. 19). These findings, one three years and the other five years after the publication of *Better Behaviour – Better Learning*, suggest that teachers, in their perceptions of and approaches to addressing behaviour in classrooms, do not constitute a coherent group. However, where Munn *et al.* (2004) and Wilkin *et al.* (2006) concur is in reporting considerable agreement among teachers in both primary and secondary schools on the debilitating effect of constant low-level disruption. If talking out of turn, interrupting other pupils and leaving a seat without permission are still problematic, then an explanation and solution must be sought beyond what is currently happening in those classrooms where young people's behaviour is perceived as difficult. Explanations for the persistent existence of unwanted behaviour range from a divergence between the values of schools and those of wider society (Munn *et al.*, 2004, p. 24; Wilkin *et al.*, 2006, p. 37) and the perceived impact of the inclusion agenda itself (Munn *et al.*, 2004, p. 33; Wilkin *et al.*, 2006, p. 37). As one participant put it: 'Social inclusion is having a severe effect on the notion of indiscipline with more serious, threatening and complicated incidents. This has a serious effect on other pupils' (Munn *et al.*, 2004, p. 32).

In the section dealing with secondary schools in Munn *et al.*'s (2004) report, teachers and head teachers were given the opportunity to express their views on exclusion. Exclusion, it was argued by participants, 'was viewed as unsuccessful, or at best neutral, for the pupil so sanctioned' (Munn *et al.*, 2004, p. 31). It was also perceived, however, that exclusion provided respite for teachers and other pupils, whilst sending a signal about behaviour to pupils and parents. When asked what would improve discipline in schools, secondary head teachers identified a change in teaching styles as the most likely effective measure. This view was at odds with that of classroom teachers in both secondary and primary schools, a sizeable minority of whom felt that increased support from senior staff in the form of communications with pupils about what they can and cannot do was their preferred option (Munn *et al.*, 2004, pp. 57, 60).

Again, this finding suggests that there is not one coherent view among teachers regarding approaches to the discipline of young people whose behaviour some of them may find difficult. There are traces of the tendency to marginalise, patronise and demonise argued in the opening chapter. Most obviously, these lie in the acceptance of exclusion as an appropriate means of dealing with some behaviours and in the strength of the language used to critique inclusion (Munn *et al.*, 2004, pp. 54 and 55) where teachers describe difficult pupils as 'stealing' other pupils' time and inclusion being 'the rod which will break the back of our education system'. In addition, the decision whether or not behaviour is perceived as disruptive or wearing and the perception that even low-level disruption is still a significant problem belong with the teacher and varies from teacher to teacher.

As with the study considered at the beginning of this chapter (Head *et al.*, 2003; Kane *et al.*, 2004), there may be a gap between what teachers perceive as effective and their preferences in dealing with difficult behaviour.

The possibility of a gap between teachers' aspirations and the systems through which they operate can be seen again in the most recent report on behaviour in Scotland's schools (Wilkin *et al.*, 2006). Most significantly, perhaps, this study indicates that a majority of teachers would prefer to deal with young people as learners rather than as behavioural 'problems' (Wilkin *et al.*, 2006, pp. vii, 95). In response to an invitation to indicate which approaches would increase their confidence in dealing with behavioural issues in their classrooms, the majority of teachers (85% secondary and 91% primary) indicated that understanding of individual pupil's learning styles and motivation would most increase their confidence. However, in response to a question regarding approaches which they felt to be the most helpful in behaviour management, 71% of teachers indicated that rules and rewards for pupils was most helpful, with a further 17% citing pupil support bases as helpful. Thus, on the one hand, teachers expressed a desire to address pupils' learning, with the accompanying implications of inclusion, at least in terms of pupils remaining within classrooms. On the other hand, however, they cited measures that address behaviour as a prerequisite to dealing with learning, or that involve pupils being taught in segregated provision, as being the most helpful approaches to dealing with behaviour.

In one sense, therefore, despite the introduction of a range of initiatives such as Staged Intervention, Restorative Practices and Solution Oriented Schools, teachers' experience of dealing with difficult children had not changed much since the beginning of the century and the implementation of the presumption of mainstreaming contained within the Standards in Scotland's Schools etc. Act 2000, followed by the policy document *Better Behaviour – Better Learning* (SEED, 2001) a year later. Possible explanations for any delay in change might include a natural conservatism and a desire to hang on to those measures that have traditionally been seen as effective, the perception of new initiatives and their accompanying demands on time and resources as additional to teachers' existing workload and, pertaining to both of these reasons, the type of professional development on offer for teachers (Wilkin *et al.*, 2006, pp. 80, 98).

The issue of staff development occupied the thoughts of participants in both the 2004 and 2006 reports. Although Continued Professional Development (CPD) was not addressed directly in 2004, teachers and head teachers nevertheless identified guidance and support from local authorities, which presumably includes the provision of CPD, as a priority. At the same time, they had rated this same measure as ineffective in helping them address behaviour in their schools and classrooms (Munn *et al.*, 2004, p. 64). In the 2006 survey, both local authority participants and teachers and support staff in schools pointed to the importance of staff development as a measure of providing effective support for staff in schools. However, criticisms of CPD currently available included claims that it needed to be more practical and proactive, and, in the case of additional support staff, specific to their needs (Wilkin *et al.*, 2006, p. 107). Much of the CPD on offer in 2006 centred on the three major initiatives that were running in schools, namely Staged Intervention, Restorative Practices and Solution Oriented Schools. Teachers' and support staff's perceived ineffectiveness of available CPD calls into question the nature of the development and how it is presented to teachers. If these initiatives are perceived as things that teachers might do *in addition* to what they already do, then teachers and support staff are unlikely to be enthusiastic in their uptake. Moreover, much of what happens in solution focused practices and restorative justice practices can be seen as happening outside the classroom and, therefore, not immediately relevant to teachers and classroom support staff in their routine work with pupils. Even in the case of Staged Intervention, in which the first two stages focus on the classroom, some teachers might see it as a threat or consider it patronising that someone should come into their classroom and 'tell them how to do their job'. Moreover, if the CPD available is largely provided for those members of staff who will become behaviour coordinators, once again, classroom teachers may see it as irrelevant for them. It is possible, therefore, that in addition to marginalising young people who may be experiencing behavioural difficulties, the measures put in place to address difficult behaviour may inadvertently be serving to patronise and marginalise teachers and support staff.

If this is the case, then an opportunity to support the development of all staff in schools is being lost. It is one thing to train a limited number of staff to be behaviour coordinators, restorative teachers or practitioners of solution-focused approaches to dealing with behaviour. It is a much more extensive exercise, however, and one that is argued in the next chapter is both desirable and necessary, for all staff in schools to be afforded the opportunity to become engaged with each of these initiatives in such a way that allows them to examine the processes and language involved in each of them and consider how they can take what they learn from them into their own classrooms. In this way, every teacher can become solution focused, restorative in their approach and thus more able to analyse their own classroom context and generate effective solutions to any problems that might arise.

The scope of the 2006 survey was widened to include pupils and their responses provide an interesting slant on what has taken place in Scotland's schools. First, whilst pupils have similar views to teachers on the effectiveness of rewards and punishments, there is a sense of perceived imbalance among pupils. Whilst they also saw punishment of indiscipline as effective, they felt that good behaviour went unrewarded. In line with teachers and support staff, they reported that exclusion of pupils who misbehave to segregated provision allowed respite for other pupils. Significantly, however, the pupil participants in the research were more severe than adult participants in their call for punishment of those pupils who misbehave. Measures suggested by pupils as effective included physical punishment and other punishments designed to humiliate, shame or embarrass those who misbehave (Wilkin *et al.*, 2006, pp. 85–7). A first response to this data might be to question the kind of young people our education system contributes towards producing. It may be, however, that the pupils' views reflected and exaggerated the opinions they assimilated from their classroom experiences. It should not be surprising, therefore, that young people raised on a diet of reward and punishment, patronising, demonising and marginalising, should themselves adopt these values within the context of school. These harsh views, however, were tempered with the same pupils' pleas for fairness, for equality and consistency of treatment by teachers for all pupils. Moreover, there was a recognition among pupils that teaching styles and practices can have an impact on behaviour and they identified 'more enjoyable lessons', 'shorter, less boring explanations' and 'more practical interactive opportunities' as measures they would find particularly effective in eliminating unwanted behaviour. In this way, pupils have reproduced the same dichotomy as teachers. On the one hand, they want behaviour dealt with in punitive ways as a precursor to learning whilst on the other hand they recognise that effective teaching, that has a clear focus on learning, reduces the opportunities for unwanted behaviour.

All of the research considered in this chapter indicates that measures to promote educational inclusion through the reduction of exclusions and the promotion of positive behaviour has led schools to look for new and innovative ways of working with young people who may be experiencing social, emotional and behavioural difficulties (Head *et al.*, 2003; Lloyd *et al.*, 2003). In addition, the various initiatives have resulted in schools and teachers considering different ways of addressing behaviour and providing support for pupils whom they find difficult to teach (Kane *et al.*, 2004). Indeed, Wilkin *et al.* (2006, p. 79) describe the range of approaches used as 'an array of different and, often inventive, approaches to managing behaviour'. However, there remain concerns that levels of pupil indiscipline are high and that any support for pupils has been gained negatively. That is to say, that as the result of being badly behaved, difficult pupils receive undue teacher attention (Wilkin *et al.*, 2006) or are dealt with as part of the school discipline system rather than as part of a pastoral care programme for all pupils, perhaps targeted at the most vulnerable young learners (Lloyd *et al.*, 2003). Consequently, the impact of inclusion has been to replicate 'special' provision within our mainstream schools in the form of bases, units and other out-of-class teaching favoured over approaches and strategies apparently perceived as more effective but that entail 'difficult' young people being in class with their well-behaved peers (Head *et al.*, 2003; Lloyd *et al.*, 2003; Munn *et al.*, 2004; Wilkin *et al.*, 2006). This has been the case particularly in what might be described as 'traditional' locations for behavioural difficulties, namely with boys, especially those from poorer families living in areas of deprivation. Young people looked after and accommodated in local authority homes and those with other disabilities such as autism and attention deficit hyperactivity disorder also feature highly among students considered to have behavioural difficulties (Lloyd *et al.*, 2003; Watson, 2000).

The difficulties with this situation are twofold. Firstly, as a direct consequence of teachers' focus being directed towards dealing with behaviour, the desired developments in pedagogies that would lead to an improved educational experience for all pupils as a result of teachers having to reassess how they taught have not yet materialised (Hanko, 2003). Secondly, hoped-for reduction in exclusions was never achieved. Indeed, the Scottish Executive's own figures indicate that inclusion initiatives have not led to any reduction in exclusions for discipline and teachers themselves report a perceived increase in classroom indiscipline (Munn *et al.*, 2004).

Head *et al.* (2003) noted that the schools in which their study was carried out were highly flexible in their approach to dealing with students felt to be difficult and that the range of responses developed reflected the diversity of difficulties experienced by students. Schools in which behaviour was clearly considered to be a matter of discipline (Kane *et al.*, 2004) relied more heavily on strategies such as punishment exercises and the setting up of 'sin-bins'. However, and within the context of social justice, the researchers identified a desire to create 'supportive relationships amongst children, staff and parents' (Head *et al.*, 2003, p. 39) in those schools where inappropriate behaviour was dealt with as a learning difficulty. Flexibility, collaboration and tenacity emerge as key themes in the wider literature on inclusion and the education of young people who may be experiencing social, emotional and behavioural difficulties (Ainscow *et al.*, 2000; Lloyd *et al.*, 2003).

If research has highlighted possible dichotomies or contradictions between the desire to address the learning of young people and the imperative to deal with their behaviour first, then it might be pertinent to ask if there is more that research can do that might generate insight into how to resolve these apparent disparities. A first step in answering this question, might be to consider what the research discussed in this chapter *has* and *has not* done. Each of the research exercises has considered the educational experience of our most troubled and troublesome children and young people largely from the point of view of the adult world. The 2006 survey and Head *et al.* (2003) and Kane *et al.* (2004) did include young people as participants, but they did so in response to the adults' questions and in a context prepared by the adults. Each of the surveys addressed the questions posed by either local or national government and the research instruments used to gather data were created by adult researchers in response to the issues occupying government. In other words, participants, whether adults or young people, could only respond within the context created for them by constraints of the research exercise. This criticism could, of course, be levelled at any research activity and is not meant to imply any weakness or undue bias in any of the research used in this chapter. Rather the matter is raised only to highlight the limitations of any piece of research and the care with which potential users of that research, teachers and local authorities in this instance, should approach the contents of reports. There may be a tendency among inexperienced users of research to assume that because something appears in a rigorously prepared and executed piece of work, that it somehow becomes irrefutable. An example of this might be teachers' perceived usefulness and effectiveness of behaviourist approaches to managing pupils' behaviour that each of the reports contains. An uncritical reader might understand this to mean that because it is perceived within the constraints of the research to be effective, that it is indeed effective, that it will work in all circumstances, and is adopted without question. Quite obviously, this is not the case.

There remains therefore, the question of what existing research has not done. Most obviously, it is not known if any of the above work has asked the questions that the participants might have wanted to ask, nor is it even certain that any of the researches addressed the themes and issues that teachers, support assistants and young people might have considered to be the most important. Sheehy (2005) argues that inclusion has taken us into a new research context. In particular, he argues that inclusive research goes beyond consideration of the interactions between researchers and participants. Instead he argues that if inclusive education seeks to achieve an educational context in which learning is for all then it may be the case that an inclusive research approach might entail the research process itself being in the hands of those being researched. Furthermore, he continues, the primary beneficiaries of research should be the researched group. In none of the above exercises was the research in the hands of the teachers or young people and certainly, they are only likely to benefit indirectly from it as the result of policy initiatives that result from the research. The direct beneficiaries are likely to be the government bodies who commissioned the research. It may well be incumbent on researchers and those who commission research in the future to conceptualise their work differently and in ways that include the researched in a much more proactive way. If the forthrightness of the young people involved in the 2006 survey is indicative, then any such research in the future might just produce more direct and relevant data.

Another thing that research has not done is investigate and resolve the contradictions that have arisen within it. In particular, the difference between teachers' wishes to deal with behavioural difficulties as part of learning and the imperative to exclude has not been explored. In addition, it is possible that research that has focused on issues of policy initiated by local and national governments has by its very nature preferred approaches favoured by these bodies. For example, the range of CPD currently on offer to teachers and support staff is largely based on the three major initiatives of Staged Intervention, Solution Oriented/focused training and Restorative Practices or approaches that address behaviour (Wilkin *et al.*, 2006, p. 107), whereas in each of the research reports considered, there was a recognition among teachers that measures that address learning are effective. This dichotomy is reflected in the findings of the 2006 report:

> The vast majority of teachers already felt confident in their ability to promote positive behaviour and deal with indiscipline in their classroom. Understanding individual pupils' learning styles and motivations was the approach thought by teachers to be most likely to increase their confidence (personal safety training was deemed least likely).
>
> Local authority interviewees considered approaches such as Staged Intervention/FFI to be effective means of responding to

indiscipline at a local authority level, as well as a comprehensive CPD menu; integrated working amongst agencies; a clear inclusion policy; and inclusion training. Effective approaches at a school and classroom level were: pupil support bases; alternative, flexible and appropriate curriculum; additional support / behaviour support staff; and Assertive Discipline. (Wilkin *et al.*, 2006, p. vii)

In the first paragraph the findings indicate that learning and not behaviour is the priority for teachers. As a result, they are seeking to develop practice in a way that helps them deal with difficulties in the classroom as part of the *process* of teaching and learning. The second paragraph, however, reveals that the preferred approach of local authority participants was to deal with behaviour as a matter of *systems* employed primarily to address behaviour. This difference between preferred approaches might also go some way to explaining both the kind of CPD available and the perception of it as ineffective.

In short, for teachers it is a question of what they do in their classrooms: how teaching is organised, how learning is facilitated, and how they interact with pupils. In other words, it is a matter of teachers' beliefs about learning and behaviour and the dispositions they have towards learners, colleagues and others involved in the learning of the young people whom they teach. For them, everything that happens in classrooms is a matter of pedagogy, which is the subject of the next chapter.

Chapter 5

TEACHER IDENTITY, PUPIL IDENTITY AND PEDAGOGY

'Pedagogy' is a term that is often used loosely and usually as a synonym for teaching. In this chapter, however, it is used more holistically to encompass everything that informs and impacts on what happens in a classroom. As such it will include teachers' personal and professional beliefs, especially regarding behaviour and learning. It will also incorporate the theories of behaviour and learning that explain and help us to understand what takes place between teachers and learners in school classrooms. The focus for much of this chapter in terms of both analysis and proposition, therefore, is the experience of teachers in classrooms.

The professional behaviour of teachers can be described largely in cognitive terms: the preparation and presentation of work for students, assessment of students and their own work, and the development of teaching and learning resources. In addition, the concept of emotional labour has recently emerged as significant in the literature concerning professional practice and development in a range of professions and the implications of the concept of emotional labour for teachers is considered as a way of understanding the circumstances in which teachers find they work. The teacher's experience provides the foundations of pedagogy that both generates and reflects the relationships between teachers and pupils that grow out of the beliefs, dispositions and theories that impact on teachers' identity as teachers. In this chapter, the arguments contained in previous chapters concerning policy, theory and research are brought together to explore ways in which they impact on teachers' work in classrooms. Finally, a mediational style of teaching is suggested as one possible means of constructing both teacher and pupil identities that relate to effective learning, and as one possible means of supporting teachers to deal with the learning of all young people in a way that does not demonise, patronise or marginalise either the pupils or their teachers.

In chapter 2 it was argued that theories that explain both pupil and teacher behaviour can be represented as a continuum stretching from behaviourist and authoritarian on the one side to humanist and democratic on the other. Similarly, how teachers teach and, consequently, how students learn, can be explained in terms of different understandings concerning the nature of knowledge and how we come to know it.

The starting point for examining conceptions of learning is ontology and its relationship to epistemology. There is much debate in the philosophical literature concerning these concepts and the complex metaphysical processes and interactions between the two that entail the generation of knowledge. For the purposes of this chapter I use them almost as defining terms in order to explore how our conceptualisations of knowledge lead to the construction of particular pedagogies. Ontology is essentially the study of being, of what entities exist. In educational terms, therefore, I take this to mean *what there is to know*. Epistemology is the theory of knowledge and how we come to know that it exists in reality. In educational terms, therefore, I take this to mean *how we come to know*. It is our beliefs about what there is to know and how we come to know it that determines what we do in classrooms; the relationships we establish between teachers and learners, the relationship between learners and the subjects being taught, and how we teach the subject material.

There are different beliefs concerning ontology, but in this chapter I concentrate only on two: those of a realist ontology and those of a relativist ontology. A realist ontology assumes that there is a fixed body of knowledge that is required to be learned. How that knowledge is learned, epistemology, is further based on the assumption that the teacher, being older, wiser and more experienced, is the expert on that body of knowledge and it is the teacher's job to connect learners with the body of knowledge. Being the authority on knowledge, the teacher, therefore, is able to decide which parts of the body of are best suited to the students' needs and transmits that knowledge to them. Therefore, in a classroom in which teaching and learning can be understood as being informed by a realist ontology, teaching is likely based on an 'expert', transmission model and the overall pedagogy to be largely behaviourist.

It follows that it is highly likely that where learning is dealt with in a behaviourist manner, student behaviour that is considered to be difficult will be treated in a similar fashion. Just as what is to be known about the world is fixed, so what is to be known about pupils will be fixed, including personal traits and behaviours. Moreover, it is also likely to be the case that students, familiar with a behaviourist regime, will expect to experience authoritarian treatment in both their learning and personal development. The same behaviourist theories predict, and the prediction can be confirmed in the research studied in Chapter 4, that in such circumstances learners are likely to be passive, lack a sense of agency and control in their learning and wider school life and when novelty evaporates from either a topic or approach to behaviour, they are liable to lose interest and revert to the unwanted behaviours that confirm their demonised, patronised and marginalised identities.

Furthermore, in schools and classrooms where this is the case, the teachers themselves can become demonised as ineffective or bad teachers. Moreover, those teachers who are perceived as being 'good at dealing with difficult children' often find themselves steered into working in segregated provision such as bases, units and special schools, or find that they have a greater number of difficult children in their classes. As a result of operating under circumstances that can be understood as being informed by realist ontology and explained by behaviourist theories, some teachers, as well as some pupils, can find themselves demonised, patronised and marginalised.

In schools where the prevailing ethos can be understood in terms of a realist ontology, the approach to dealing with young people's behaviour is likely to be similarly founded on behaviourist principles that assume deficit on the child's part. Regardless of their personal beliefs, teachers working in predominantly behaviourist environments will be encouraged to perceive certain pupil behaviours as 'indiscipline' and address them as part of the school discipline procedures.

Dealing with difficult behaviour as a matter of discipline may appear to be the obvious approach but it has disadvantages as well as benefits. Typically, methods of dealing with behaviour that is perceived as disruptive are couched in terms of 'assertive discipline' (Canter and Canter, 1992) or 'positive behaviour' in its many forms (e.g. Drifte, 2004). These approaches are popular in schools as they recognise the teacher's right to establish order on students and the use of rewards and sanctions allows undesirable behaviour to be targeted and replaced by more acceptable behaviour (Ayers *et al.*, 2000; Porter, 2000). Moreover, by having a clear focus on behaviour, it is easier for both teacher and pupil to understand which behaviours are being addressed and the rewards or sanctions they will attract. However, the major difficulty with such approaches is that whilst they can have an immediate impact on behaviour, their effectiveness is likely to diminish in the long term, usually as the reward loses its sense of novelty or the sanction becomes perceived by the pupil as ineffective. A positive behaviour approach addresses behaviour rather than the causes of behaviour and, therefore, is less likely to have any long-term effect (Garner and Gains, 1996).

Other approaches argue that unacceptable behaviour is the result of events and interactions in a complex matrix of relationships that involve pupils, teachers, schools and parents and that 'disruptions occur when students' emotional or relationship needs are not being met' (Porter, 2000, p. 11). The principal attractiveness of what might be called democratic approaches to behaviour is that they suggest that we should tackle the causes of behaviour rather than simply the behaviour itself. Problems with such approaches are that they may involve teachers undertaking additional training (e.g. in solution-focused approaches) and they require a sharing of control over what takes place in the classroom. Moreover, and more importantly, many of the developments suggested are allied to the introduction of novelty programmes and may entail teachers becoming involved in activities beyond what might be considered as teaching and learning: for example, developing a pupil profile as part of a nurture group process.

Other guidance that has a focus on what teachers already do as its starting point (e.g. Gray, 2002; Porter, 2000) tends to explore the relationships among pupils, parents and teachers and what the implications of these relationships are for learning and teaching. Even here, though, there is an underlying assumption that once the relationship is sorted, 'appropriate' behaviour will ensue and, consequently, learning will take place. In other words, there are two propositions inherent in the argument; firstly, the first step is to deal with the behaviour (by dealing with the cause); and secondly, that thereafter, learning will, quite naturally, take place. Moreover, there is little or no explicit exploration of what constitutes appropriate behaviour or what the class teacher in everyday lessons in ordinary classes in primary and secondary schools might do as part of their standard teaching practice to address the causes of difficult behaviour in a way that ensures that learning is taking place. Rayner (1998) suggests that appropriate behaviour is equivalent to learning behaviour and that is the focus of the later parts of this chapter.

As recognised in previous chapters, schools have adopted a range of approaches and programmes aimed at supporting young people. One effect of this innovation has been the development of what has been termed an affective curriculum (Hanko, 2003): that is, ways of interacting with students that recognise the importance of feelings and emotions in the learning process (Gray, 2002; Watkins and Wagner, 2000). Implicit in these approaches is the recognition that behavioural difficulties are a social construct: that they emerge as the result of interactions between teachers and pupils or among pupils and that they are linked, therefore, 'to the quality of the day-to-day educational experience of pupils and their teachers' (Hanko, 2003, p. 126). Core to the improvement of such experiences is the recognition that all participants have an important role to play, that each feels valued and that they belong and that the expectations and goals of education authorities and schools match those of their students and teachers (Cooper et al., 2000; Head, 2003).

However, in schools as they exist, an inherent difficulty with developing a curriculum that addresses the affective domain of the mind, based on equity, lies in the possibility that it may, in fact, conflict with the subject or cognitive curriculum, particularly in how it is taught. Hanko (2003), Lloyd et al. (2003) and Maclellan and Soden (2003) all recognise that teachers' own experiences of school and learning might be quite different from that within which they are being asked to operate. Most teachers' learning will have been through a didactic, transmission modality in which learning is teacher directed, content and pace are decided by the teacher and the majority of learning is deemed to take place as the result of teacher exposition and student listening. This context closely resembles the six observations made by Watson (2000) that lead to difficulties within the learning environment. Consequently, when asked to address the learning of young people whom they perceive as unable or unwilling to participate in the learning process as described, teachers find that it takes up an inordinate amount of their time to the detriment of their other pupils and that they lack the training and expertise to deal with some young learners (Hanko, 2003). Where support has been provided in the form of a behaviour support colleague, there can be a sense in which the effectiveness of the support is felt to be limited by the inability of the support teacher to provide teaching informed by subject knowledge, skills and understanding (Head *et al.*, 2003).

However, in schools in which learning and teaching can be understood in terms of relativist ontology, the experience of teachers and pupils is quite different. The assumptions underpinning a relativist ontology include the belief that knowledge is not fixed but is dynamic, organic and contextualised socially and culturally. For teachers who operate within an environment understood by a relativist ontology, instead of there being one 'truth' to be taught as an orthodoxy, there are a range of ways of understanding and making sense of the world that await to be discovered. Epistemologically, knowledge is the product of the interactions among communities, groups and individuals in ways that make meaning in the cultural and social contexts of learners and their teachers. Thus scientists will argue that what we know about the way in which our world functions is only temporary until new knowledge is generated. Similarly, views on world affairs will be constructed differently in different cultures resulting, for example, in the different approaches to issues such as global warming, whale fishing and the development of nuclear energy adopted by various governments and interested groups. In classrooms, a relativist ontology translates into how knowledge is considered as relevant and important not in the view of an expert but in the social and cultural contexts of the learners. Knowledge, therefore, is constructed socially. Pedagogy in classrooms that can be understood in terms of relativism is more likely to reflect the theories of Vygotsky, Piaget and the philosophies of those who advocate critical pedagogies and democratic schools. Examples of relativist pedagogies would include Etienne Wenger's concept of communities of practice (Wenger, 1998) and activity theory as developed by Yrjo Engeström (Engeström *et al.*, 1999). Just as behaviour in classes that can be understood in terms of behaviourist theories is likely to be dealt with in an authoritarian manner; in classes informed by relativist theories, the focus of attention is more likely to be on learning rather than behaviour and behaviour is understood and dealt with in terms of learning. Thus, there is a close correlation between humanist theories of behaviour and relativist, social constructivist theories of learning.

Whilst theories explain the teaching and learning in classrooms, the interactions between teachers and students construct the identity of both. In education, we often talk of the process of learning and, in particular, the processes involved in progress whether that be in learning, performance or behaviour. In each case, we tend to visualise progress as linear and make assumptions that once a certain point has been reached, there is no going back. Even where we expect peaks and troughs we assume that the momentum gained will propel us in an otherwise steadily forward course. Often, as students move along the line of progress they are rewarded. Similarly, if there are setbacks they meet with consequences such as, in the case of behaviour, loss of privileges or punishment.

However, those teachers, classroom assistants and other support workers involved in supporting young people when their learning, or more especially, behaviour may require the provision of additional support, know that progress does not take place in uniformly straight lines. Their experience is more likely to include development that can go forwards, backward, up and down. To expect linear progress is, therefore, both unrealistic and sets unfair expectations on students and their teachers. Instead, if working with children and young people is visualised as comprising a series of multidirectional movements that take on the meaning that students' and teachers' experiences bring to them, then the development, the progress in terms of expanded experience, becomes visible to both teacher and learner rather than hidden under a series of successes and failures, rewards and punishments. The implications of working in this way can be illustrated by an example of a regime based on humanist principals, social constructivist theory and a philosophy of Otherness. The example concerned the inclusion of school refusers in a large secondary school in the west of Scotland (Head and Jamieson, 2006). Analysis of the regime revealed that behaviour support teachers in the school had designed a system of non-threatening and democratic support (which they termed a protocol) based on the development of behaviours in the young people whom they were supporting.

In psychological terms, the overall approach could be categorised as one of exposure (Lauchlan, 2003). However, the operation of the support given differed from the normal expectations of similar approaches. Exposure can be described as a cognitive-behavioural technique in which the child's exposure to school is gradually increased until they are 'attending school normally for an agreed number of mornings or afternoons per week, culminating in full return to school over time' (Lauchlan, 2003, p. 140). The argument for this approach is based on the premise that the longer pupils do not come to school, the more they will fall behind in their work and the more difficult they will find it to return. This argument was recognised in the support provided for the young people. Normally, an exposure approach would have built-in progression with attendance becoming increasingly longer. These periods of attendance would be negotiated in advance, probably the subject of some kind of 'contract' and monitoring by both the student and the school. Support operating in this way can be understood in terms of behaviourist theories and realist ontology.

However, the support provided in this case can be understood in humanist and democratic terms. Firstly, there were no contracts or pre-agreed goals or standards set. Moreover, there was an in-built recognition that progress is not linear. In addition, although praise, encouragement and reward were specifically identified by staff as possible motivators, there was no mention of extrinsic rewards from any of the participants.

In another research project (Lang *et al.*, 1998 cited in Lauchlan, 2003) involving two groups of school refusers, one of which received intensive positive reinforcement whilst the other received none over a 12-week period, the researchers found no difference between the two forms of intervention. Lang's study and the one discussed here are small scale but both suggest that purely psychological explanations, whilst useful in analysing what is taking place and how it works or does not work are limited in the extent to which they can adequately explain why specific interventions work in particular contexts.

In order to reach a satisfactory explanation of why this particular approach was felt to work, a re-conception of the problem was required. Psychologically, the difficulty was understood as one of inadequacy within the child: some children were unable to come to school or classes, therefore the underlying emotional or social circumstances that caused them to absent themselves from school needed to be addressed. Crucially, in this case, the problem was conceptualised as a difficulty of learning and the main aim became reconnecting the learner with learning rather than the 'sorting' of circumstances that may have been inhibiting learning.

Essentially, this was a matter of identity and the power relationships that exist within schools. Each of the young people involved had constructed an identity for themselves that was related to their reasons for non-attendance. This identity was reinforced through surveillance by the school, teachers and most importantly, their fellow pupils. In most cases the young people involved were able to pinpoint a particular circumstance that led to their refusal to go to school. In each case, the effect of this circumstance was reinforced by their experiences of being in school or their projected assumptions of what that experience might be. Two of the students specifically mentioned being looked at and talked about by other pupils and all at some point made reference to teachers and adults talking to or about them in a particular way either as part of classroom interactions or within meetings. The overall psychological effect of this was to render the young people feeling that within school they were under constant surveillance, always of a negative nature, either by their peers or teachers. Pupils spoke of the effect of looking and being looked at and the power of looking was recognised in the protocol developed by the support teachers. Sartre argues that being looked at captures us and creates an identity for us that is inapprehensible to us but which makes us its prisoner:

I am possessed by the Other; the Other's look fashions my body in its nakedness, causes it to be born, sculptures it, produces it as it is, sees it as I shall never see it. The Other holds a secret – the secret of what I am. (Sartre, 1969, p. 364)

Jay (1993), in his explication of Sartre's work on the tension between perception and imagination in relationship to the gaze, offers a way into an explanation of why this might be the case in this instance. Jay, following Sartre, explains that to perceive is to 'look at', thus rendering the person being looked at as the object of the gaze. However, the person being looked at is in a passive role, only conscious of being looked upon. In this instance, the pupils' imagination interpreted the gaze in terms of their underlying problem, reporting even (whether real or imaginary) that others were talking about them. Thus the pupils unable to apprehend what lay behind the looking created their own interpretation, thus rendering themselves subject to 'the paralyzing internalization of the other's gaze' (Jay, 1993, p. 288). Jay goes on to argue that the relationship between the subject and object is one of power in which the one who is being looked at is constantly turned into an object. However, as the object identifies with the other's look (through imagination) they then place themselves in the position of subject and the self 'is replaced by a self that is constituted by the gaze of the other' (Jay, 1993, p. 288). Thus the pupils in this case ceased to identify themselves as students and learners and instead, through a process of subjectivity, created an identity related to their non-attendance at school.

This identity as subject who does not belong can be reinforced by the relationships that exist within some schools. Cummins (2003) argues that the dominant, powerful groups within education construct the differences that children bring to school as deficits and explanations for their poor performance. Moreover, the coercive power relations that exist within wider society are reflected in the hierarchical structures of schools, thereby situating the relationship between teacher and pupil within a context of power in which the pupil is in a state of subjectification as a result of constant surveillance by school, teacher and peers. In addition, the materials of school— subject areas, timetables, books and other materials—also construct subjectivity. In a critique of Montessori's management of attention, Sobe (2004, p. 295) argues that they represent 'strategies for organizing human perception that rely upon a theorization of attention as deliberate, cultivated, and affirmative of certain truths about the subject'. In this instance, the 'certain truths' belonged to the students' identities as school refusers.

The lived experience of the young people involved, of always being the target of the gaze, served to reinforce the identity constructed by those looking, at least within their own imagination. Jay (1993, p. 400) points out that Foucault was 'interested in the non-relationship between the visible and the sayable', a non-relationship that takes on the properties of a relationship when the young people, aware of being looked at and talked about interpret their experience in terms of language.

Significantly, the behaviour support staff were aware that looking at a pupil can be interpreted by the pupil as threatening and, as part of the protocol, deliberately created contexts where they did not have to, or could not, look directly at pupils. This was a crucial first step in creating the context in which pupils did not feel under surveillance and consequent subjectification. By modifying this aspect of teacher–pupil interaction the student was able to begin the process of deconstructing an identity related to the reasons for non-attendance.

Moreover, a shift in identity was facilitated by the support staff's use of language. In particular, how both speech and silence were conceptualised as part of a continuum of communication in which they complement each other (Zembylas and Michaelides, 2004). Traditionally, silence is not always valued in classrooms, is interpreted as insolence, ignorance or defiance, and the 'silencing of silence' becomes a matter of control and discipline. In such a context 'silence itself can easily regress into a regime of subjectification' (Zembylas and Michaelides, 2004, p. 202). However, silence was used quite differently in this context.

The protocol of support involved collecting pupils by car. The fact that the drivers must concentrate on the road means that their gaze is directed away from the student. Driving has the additional advantage that concentration on traffic can also curtail conversation and the tendency for the adults to fill the silence with their speech. Moreover, the support staff recognised the importance of silence as an act of communication. The teachers' approach of 'gentle persuasion' mentioned by pupils is an indication that the support staff recognised that, from the pupil's point of view, efforts to persuade them to go to classes could feel threatening. Likewise, pupil observations that they could 'sit quiet and do my work' and an example of support staff language, 'I hope this thing stops and you can go by yourself' are further examples of how language and silence were used. Explicit language is suggestive rather than persuasive, but support staff's patience in not demanding verbal responses is a clear recognition that silence and other non-verbal communication are important elements of classroom interaction. The subject of returning to class is an emotional one for the pupils concerned and since 'the majority of students' emotional communications take place without talk' (Zembylas and Michaelides, 2004, p. 200), then to subject pupils to spoken language aimed at persuasion by trying to voice the unspeakable, would, in fact, be likely to be self-defeating. Rather, support staff's conduct was a recognition that sometimes some things cannot be said and that in these contexts, speech is limited and that silence itself becomes part of the pedagogical process. When silence is conceptualised in this way, as part of a communicative process that includes speech and other non-verbal communication, then it is also possible to move beyond the instrumental use of silence as a time for reflection, or as wait time before expecting an answer. Instead, silence can be seen as having intrinsic pedagogical merits that 'can be conducive for both teachers and students to raise awareness of here and now and invite them to enter the mindful process of self-criticality' (Zembylas and Michaelides, 2004, p. 202).

The approach adopted by support staff in this instance was one based on modesty. Whilst on a personal level there may have been a desire to understand what was going on in the pupils' heads and to sort thing out for them, support staff were aware that this was impossible. Such an approach would be about the adult and what the adult can do. The approach used here was about the pupil and was contained within the common ground on which the relationship between the adults and young people was founded, the young people's learning. Zembylas and Michaelides compare this to '"teaching with ignorance" because it is through silence and ignorance (unknowability) that one stops laying claim to another's experience and begins to be receptive to the Other' (Zembylas and Michaelides, 2004, p. 207). The process as it operates in this context is similar to that described in a study of a range of discourses on school non-attendance in Japan (Yoneyama, 2000) in which the experience of school refusers was represented as a process in which they are compelled to address a number of questions concerning themselves. Prime among these is one of identity and, Yoneyama argues, only when students have deconstructed the identities created for them by others and reconstructed their own identities in contrast to those others, are they able to resume a life of social interaction. Indicative of the significance of identity in all of this, and evidenced in the example studied above, is that whilst shifting identity can result in positive change, the underlying psychological 'problem' may still exist. Although pupils themselves felt they no longer had anxieties and fears about coming to school, their parents and teachers still perceived signs that they were. However, because the pupils had reconstructed new identities for themselves that were not (or not solely) related to their reasons for non-attendance, then the fears themselves assumed much less importance for the students. The support staff and pupils in this school developed an approach that entailed both cognitive and affective investment and led to an understanding of how difference is created in schools and how the dominant value of normalisation can operate against the interests of the marginalised learner (Boler and Zembylas, 2003).

Another significant element of support and how it operated in this context relates to empowerment. The power relationships that exist within school have been touched on above and are based on a philosophy of schooling that is divisive in terms of age, ability, and power that preferences schools and teachers over pupils and is usually justified on the basis of equality, on the equal treatment of all pupils. For example, for the majority of pupils in any school, participation means attending all classes at all times. For pupils and staff in this study, however, participation entailed becoming actively involved in their learning. The pupils decided which classes they felt able to attend, whether or not a support assistant accompanied them and how long the assistant stayed with them in class. Le Cornu and Collins (2004) argue that when schools are prepared to adopt similar democratic structures, provide supportive relationships and have a clear focus on learning as their main priority, then they create the kind of learning culture that is more likely to include all young people. Ng (2003, p. 212) argues that equality based regimes only serve to highlight differences among pupils 'rendering [some of] them deviant in an environment that aims at standardization and uniformity'. Instead, she argues, an approach based on equity, that makes explicit and challenges the power relationships that exist in schools, would benefit everyone concerned, teachers and pupils alike. The pupils and staff in this instance worked together in a way that developed an understanding of classroom relationships and interactions that were seen in a context of equity.

What pupils and support staff achieved in this instance was similar to the de-schooling of school (Illich, 1971). An approach to support based on persuasion concerning the need to go and merits of going to school, probably accompanied by progress targets, would have served, in Illich's argument, to create a context that led to 'an increasing reliance on institutional care [that] adds a new dimension to their helplessness: psychological impotence, the inability to fend for themselves' (Illich, 1971, p. 3). Instead, the normal routines, rules and expectation of school were suspended and the focus shifted from an emphasis on participation to learning. In other words, the focus of priority shifted from the self (the school and adults) to the Other (pupils). This shift allowed the pupils to challenge and deconstruct identities of themselves based on helplessness and the reason for their absence from school. Furthermore, by providing a framework that educated them in decision-making, action and self-help, they were able to construct another identity for themselves based on learning and efficacy. Thus, paradoxically, as school was de-schooled, the pupils found themselves increasingly more able to participate in school.

The relationship between the self and the Other in a concrete context such as this, was dynamic, interactive and organic. Therefore, not only were pupils afforded the opportunity to create a new identity for themselves, but the teachers and other adults too constructed a new identity for themselves. This identity related not only to their own experience of the context but in the attitudes that developed out of their sense of themselves in the presence of their students, a different sense of themselves as teachers and support assistants (Sartre, 1969, p. 363). The focus of their activities thus shifted from what they had to do (in terms of programmes, approaches or curricula) towards what the students required to address their learning. Wittingly or otherwise, the support staff in this instance have created a pedagogy of difference in which they and their students 'seek to engage questions of social justice and alter the ideological preconditions of prejudice and discrimination' (Trifonus, 2003, p. 3) that would normally have seen them pressurised into attending all classes at all times as a matter of school discipline and control.

The learning experience of pupils in this example can be likened to what Pádraig Hogan has called the 'epiphanies' of learning (Hogan, 2005). The relationship between teachers and learners in this case was one of the teacher as one-caring and pupil as cared-for (Noddings, 2007). In this relationship, the teacher receives the student as other, 'completely and non-selectively' (Noddings, 2007, p. 372). Whilst retaining their own ethical ideals, the staff above started from a position of respect and regard for the pupils' concerns and aspirations. The role of the teacher in a caring relationship is to influence rather than instruct or discipline. In keeping with Hogan's argument, the teacher realises that regardless of what she teaches, what the pupil learns is what he makes of it, what is relevant to him, how it fits with his context, and that this takes place at some undetermined point within the pupil's psyche, when 'things come together' and make sense for whatever reason. In the example above, therefore, whenever an idea was 'suggested' or students offered the 'gentle persuasion' they described and they, in turn, responded:

> [the teacher] receive[d] not just the 'response' but the student. What he says matters, whether it is right or wrong, and she probes gently for clarification, interpretation, contribution. She is not seeking the answer but the involvement of the cared-for. (Noddings, 2007, p. 373)

In recognising the significance of the other, the teachers in the above example also recognised that the student was always more important than the subject matter or context. Moreover, their approach was informed by an optimistic view based on students' capabilities rather than any perceived deficit.

Terzi (2007) argues that a capability perspective on the learning of young people has double benefit. First, there is benefit for the value of education itself. Education becomes perceived as good in itself and as students become more educated, their chances of fulfilling a more complete and effective role in society are increased. Secondly, a capability approach is founded on the argument that education increases the repertoire of capabilities available to students by expanding both ability and opportunity. Central to this process is pedagogy (Terzi, 2007, p. 310).

The question remains, however, one of the significance and relevance of the above for the everyday subject class in any school. If the example, explanations and arguments offered so far in this chapter are to be meaningful for teachers in any learning context, including the subject classroom, then they must suggest a pedagogy that can be understood in terms of relativist ontology, is posited on capability and creates the context in which the 'epiphanies' of learning are more likely to occur. One such possibility lies within the field of metacognition and a mediational style of teaching.

Learning, behaviour and metacognition

The efficacy of metacognition in learning has been argued for some time now (Adey and Shayer, 1994; Ashman and Conway, 1997; Shayer and Adey, 2002) and its introduction into school been the subject of research (McGuiness, 1999; Wilson, 2000). There is debate about whether or not it should be taught as a discrete programme or infused in particular subject areas. Thus we have seen the appearance in schools of programmes based on the work of Reuven Feuerstein's Instrumental Enrichment (IE) (Feuerstien *et al.*, 1980), Mathew Lipman's philosophy and thinking for children (Lipman, 1988, 1993, 2003), and Robert Fisher's use of literature for children's thinking (Fisher, 1999, 2000), each of which provides a context in which learning can be addressed as a metacognitive process which is then bridged into other contexts.

At the same time, 'infused' programmes aimed at cognitive acceleration have arisen most notably in science and maths but accompanied by a slow expansion into a range of curricular areas.

The benefits of each of these programmes has been researched to greater or lesser degrees by the International Center for the Enhancement for Learning Potential (ICELP) and their effectiveness discussed in the literature (Adey and Shayer, 1994; Ashman and Conway, 1997; Head and O'Neill, 1999). However, while programmes for learners have been produced, the implications for teachers of adopting a metacognitive approach to learning have not received the same attention. The one notable exception is Carl Haywood's mediational style of teaching – which he incorporates as part of *Bright Start*, his metacognitive programme for young learners (Haywood, 1993). What may be helpful for teachers to look at is how the pedagogy inherent in a metacognitive approach to learning can be transferred into teaching in any context, thereby allowing teachers to address SEBD as a learning difficulty rather than a behavioural difficulty. In doing this, the rights of all children to learn and the right of the teacher to teach become enmeshed as part of the one process and are not seen in terms of competing rights.

Before going on to look at what one might mediate for, it might be helpful to consider what is meant by mediation and how it differs from instruction, transmission or other modes of teaching. The idea of a mediational style of teaching was developed from the work of Reuven Feuerstein and his IE programme. IE is posited on two main concepts: one of cognitive modifiability; and another of mediated learning. Feuerstein argues that the difference between a mediation and an interaction lies in how the adult intervenes between the child and the world in a way that allows the child to understand the world better. For example, an interaction might be a request such as 'Could you close the door, please.' The child can choose to grant or refuse the request on little grounds other than she or he felt like doing it or not doing it. A mediation makes this less likely by offering some grounds for carrying out the request, for example: 'Could you close the door please, there's a draught and we'll all catch cold.' Here, the teacher has introduced the notion of cause and effect and supplied a reason why the child might want to carry out the request. Children can, of course, still refuse but in doing so they are having to justify (even inwardly) why they do not hold the reason given by the teacher to be important enough or why they hold some reason for not closing the door to be more important. Even if they refuse, the teacher can take the discussion forward on the basis of the reason rather than any perceived instance of misbehaviour, thereby challenging the child's thinking process rather than their behaviour. Again, how this would be done would entail mediation within a metacognitive context so that the 'conflict' is used as a learning opportunity.

Much of what Haywood describes as mediation (Haywood, 1993) would appear familiar already as 'good practice' and this is one benefit of choosing this approach; it takes what teachers are already good at and builds on it. Haywood (1993) argues that, 'A teaching style is concerned not with only *what* one teaches but primarily *how* one teaches it' (p. 32). He then goes on to list the six most important criteria of a mediated learning experience. These are mediation for intentionality, transcendence, communication of meaning and purpose, feelings of competence, regulation of behaviour and shared participation. He then goes on to describe the most useful mediating mechanisms of process questioning, bridging, challenging or requiring justification, teaching about rules and emphasising order, predictability, system, sequence and strategies. Exactly how these are realised in the classroom is entirely down to the teacher, thereby empowering the teacher to address the learning of all the children in his or her class. Haywood recognises that, 'There are as many specific ways to mediate . . . to children as there are good mediators' (Haywood, 1993, p. 36). However, it may be advantageous to take one of his criteria and consider how it might play out in a class.

The most obvious example in the context of behaviour and learning is mediation for regulation of behaviour. This calls into question two aspects:

first, the kind of behaviour we want to mediate for and secondly, how we might create the context which not only encourages it but actively allows for it.

When faced with questions of what constitutes acceptable and unacceptable or appropriate and inappropriate behaviour, colleagues usually describe something that looks like polite and impolite behaviour, respectively. This may well be the kind of behaviour that, traditionally, we have come to argue needs to be prevalent for learning to take place. However, it does not guarantee that learning is taking place; a child might be quiet enough and busy but such behaviour may only indicate that the student is performing well and may not actually be learning (Dweck, 2000). In previous chapters it has been argued that the kind of behaviour that we might like to regulate for could be termed as learning behaviour. Again, Haywood's own criteria and the metacognitive process provide some answers.

The first sign that learning is taking place might be that the students are involved in planning behaviour. They will map out and define what they have to do and develop a strategy and tactics for doing it. The plan, strategy and tactics will be justified in terms of previous learning or a hypothesis on something as yet unknown that will be tested in the course of carrying out the task. Whilst carrying out their task, students will be reviewing their work, comparing it with the criteria for success and thereby generating the information they need to know whether or not their work is good work and what to do about it if it is not. Post task, there will be reflection on what has been learned and how it can help the student in future contexts in class, in the school and beyond. Throughout this process, the students will have been active in their own learning, generating the knowledge they need to accomplish their task, analysing success, creating strategies for dealing with difficulties and reflecting on what they have learned and its usefulness in the world at large. As well as creating the wherewithal to perform the immediate task, the students are also developing the insight and understanding that is required to justify being in the school in the first place.

Adopting a mediational style of teaching allows the teacher to commit to the student, to engage with the subject matter through the eyes, ears and mind of the student. At the same time the continuous probing and searching through process questioning, requiring justification and bridging maintains the teacher's own ethic and integrity. By generating understanding of the subject being taught from the learner's perspective, the teacher is then able to intervene between the student and the subject material in a way that helps the teacher mediate for the student and allows the student to make sense of it in both personal and generalised terms. Thus, through a mediational style of teaching, the teacher creates a learning context based on a student's capabilities, that allows the student to make the shift in identity away from that related to misbehaviour to construct another, in educational terms more powerful, identity as an effective learner. As a consequence, as students progress through gaining a deeper understanding and sense of themselves in the world, unwanted behaviour diminishes and is replaced by learning behaviour.

REFERENCES

Adey, P. and Shayer, M. (1994) *Really Raising Standards*, London: Routledge

Ainscow, M., Booth, T., Black Hawkins, K., Vaughn, M. and Shaw, L. (2000) *Index for Inclusion: Developing Learning and Participation in Schools*, Bristol: Centre for Studies in Inclusive Education

Ashman, A. F. and Conway, R. N. F. (1997) *An Introduction to Cognitive Education*, London: Routledge

Ayers, H., Clarke, D., and Murray, A. (2000) *Perspectives on Behaviour: A Practical Guide to Effective Interventions for Teachers*, London: David Fulton

Bennathan, M. and Boxall, M. (2000) *Effective Intervention in Primary Schools: Nurture Groups*, 2nd edn, London: David Fulton

Birmingham (2003) 'Behaviour in Schools: Framework for Intervention', Birmingham: Birmingham City Council Education Department (online). Available from URL: atschool. eduweb.co.uk/outlooks/Ffl.pdf (accessed 1 February 2007)

Boler, M. and Zembylas, M. (2003) 'Discomforting truths: the emotional terrain of understanding difference', in Trifonus (ed.) (2003), pp. 110–136

Bruner, J. (1996) *The Culture of Education*, Cambridge MA: Harvard University Press

Canter, L. and Canter, M. (1992) *Assertive Discipline: Positive Behaviour Management for Today's Classroom*, Santa Monica, CA: Lee Canter and Associates

Cooper, P. (1993) *Effective Schools for Disaffected Students: Integration and Segregation*, London: Routledge

Cooper, P. (1996) 'Giving it a name: the value of descriptive categories in educational approaches to emotional and behavioural difficulties', *Support for Learning*, Vol. 11, No. 4, pp. 146–150

Cooper, P., Hart, S., Lavery, J. and McLaughlin, C. (2000) *Positive Alternatives to Exclusion*, London: RoutledgeFalmer

Cummins, J. (2003) 'Challenging the construction of difference as deficit: where are identity, intellect, imagination, and power in the new regime of truth?', in Trifonus (ed.) (2003), pp. 41–60

Daniels, H., Hey, V., Leonard, D. and Smith, M. (2000) 'Issues of equity in special needs education as seen from the perspective of gender', in Daniels, H. (ed) (2000) *Special Education Re-formed. Beyond Rhetoric?* London: Falmer Press, pp. 47–66

DES (1978) *Meeting Special Educational Needs: Report of the Committee of Inquiry into the Education of Handicapped Children and Young People* (The Warnock Report), London: HMSO

Drifte, C. (2004) *Encouraging Positive Behaviour in the Early Years: A Practical Guide*, London: Paul Chapman

Dweck, C. S. (2000) *Self Theories: Their Role in Motivation, Personality, and Development*, Philadelphia: Psychology Press

Dyson, A. (2001) 'Special needs in the twenty-first century: where we've been and where we're going', *Support for Learning*, Vol. 28, No. 1, pp. 24–9

Engeström, Y., Miettinen, R. and Punamäki, R. L. (1999) *Perspectives on Activity Theory*, Cambridge: Cambridge University Press

Feuerstein, R., Rand, Y., Hoffman, M. and Miller, R. (1980) *Instrumental Enrichment: An Intervention Programme for Cognitive Modifiability*, Glenview, IL: Scott, Foresman

Fisher, R. (1999) *First Stories for Thinking*, Oxford: Nash Pollock

Fisher, R. (2000) *First Poems for Thinking*, Oxford: Nash Pollock

Galloway, D. and Goodwin, C. (1987) *The Education of Disturbing Children: Pupils with Learning and Adjustment Difficulties*, London: Longman

Gardner, H. (1993) *Frames of Mind: The Theory of Multiple Intelligences*, 2nd edn, London: Fontana

Garner, P. and Gains, C. (1996) 'Models of intervention for children with emotional and behavioural difficulties', *Support for Learning*, Vol. 11, No. 4, pp. 141–5

George, E., Iveson, C. and Ratner, H. (1999) *Problem to Solution: Brief Therapy with Individuals and Families*, London: BT Press

Giddens, A. (1994) *Beyond Left and Right: The Future of Radical Politics*, Cambridge: Polity Press

Goleman, D. (1996) *Emotional Intelligence: Why it can matter more than IQ*, London: Bloomsbury

Gray, P. (ed.) (2002) *Working with Emotions*, London: RoutledgeFalmer

Hanko, G. (2003) 'Towards an inclusive school culture – but what happened to Elton's "affective curriculum"'?, *British Journal of Special Education*, Vol. 30, No. 3, pp. 125–31

Haywood, H. C. (1993) 'A mediational teaching style', *International Journal of Cognitive Education and Mediated Learning*, Vol. 3, No. 1, pp. 27–37

Head, G. (2003) 'Effective collaboration: deep collaboration as an essential element of the learning process', Journal of Educational Enquiry, Vol. 4, No. 2, pp. 47–62 (online). Available from URL: www.literacy.unisa.edu.au/jee (accessed 1 February 2007)

Head, G. (2005) 'Better learning – better behaviour', *Scottish Educational Review*, Vol. 37, No. 2, pp. 94–103

Head, G. and Jamieson, S. (2006) 'Taking a line for a walk: including school refusers', *Pastoral Care in Education*, Vol. 24, No. 3 pp. 32–40

Head, G., Kane, J. and Cogan, N. (2002) *An Evaluation of Behaviour Support in Secondary Schools in South Lanarkshire*, Glasgow: University of Glasgow

Head, G., Kane, J. and Cogan, N. (2003) 'Behaviour support in secondary schools: what works for schools?' *Emotional and Behavioural Difficulties*, Vol. 8, No. 1, pp. 33–42

Head, G. and O'Neill, W. (1999) 'Introducing Feuerstein's Instrumental Enrichment in a school for children with social, emotional and behavioural difficulties', *Support for Learning*, Vol. 14, No. 3, pp. 122–8

Hogan, P. (2005) 'The politics of identity and the epiphanies of learning', in Carr, W. (ed.) (2005) *Philosophy of Education*, London: Routledge, pp. 83–96

Illich, I. D. (1971) *Deschooling Society*, London: Calder and Boyars

International Center for the Enhancement of Learning Potential (no date), research reports (online). Available from URL: www.icelp.org/asp/main.asp (accessed 26 March 2007)

Jay, M. ((1993) *Downcast Eyes: The Denigration of Vision in Twentieth Century French Thought*, Berkley: University of California Press

Kane, J., Head, G. and Cogan, N. (2004) 'Towards inclusion? Models of behaviour support in secondary schools in one education authority in Scotland', *British Journal of Special Education*, Vol. 31, No. 2, pp. 68–74

Kohn, A. (1996) *Beyond Discipline: from Compliance to Community*, Alexandria, VA: Association for Supervision and Curriculum Development

Lauchlan, F. (2003) 'Responding to chronic non-attendance: a review of intervention approaches', *Educational Psychology in Practice*, Vol. 19, No. 2, pp. 133–46

Le Cornu, R. and Collins, J. (2004) 'Re-emphasising the role of affect in learning and teaching', *Pastoral Care*, Vol. 24, No. 4, pp. 27–33

Lipman, M. (1988) *Philosophy Goes to School*, Philadelphia: Temple University Press

Lipman, M. (1993) *Thinking Children and Education*, Dubuque, IO: Kendall/Hunt Pub.

Lipman, M. (2003) *Thinking in Education*, 2nd edn, Cambridge: Cambrdige University Press

Lloyd, G. (2005) 'EBD girls – a critical view', in Lloyd, G. (ed.) 2005) *Problem Girls*, Abingdon: RoutledgeFalmer

Lloyd, G., Stead, J. and Kendrick, A. (2003) 'Joined up approaches to prevent school exclusion', *Emotional and Behavioural Difficulties*, Vol. 8, No. 1, pp. 77–91

Maclellan, E. and Soden, R. (2003) 'Expertise, expert teaching and experienced teachers' knowledge of learning theory', *Scottish Educational Review*, Vol. 35, No. 2, pp. 110–20

Macleod, G. (2006) 'Bad, mad or sad: constructions of young people in trouble and implications for intervention', *Emotional and Behavioural Difficulties*, Vol. 11, No. 3, pp. 155–67

Matthews, B. (2006) *Engaging Education: Developing Emotional Literacy, Equity and Co-Education*, Maidenhead: Open University Press

McGuiness, C. (1999) *From Thinking Skills to Thinking Classrooms*, Research Brief no. 115, London: DfEE

Munn, P., Lloyd, G. and Cullen, M.A. (2000) *Alternatives to Exclusion from School*, London: Paul Chapman

Munn, P., Johnstone, M. and Sharp, S. (2004) *Discipline in Scottish Schools: A Comparative Survey over Time of Teachers' and Headteachers' Perceptions*, Edinburgh: Scottish Executive

Ng, Roxana (2003) 'Toward an integrative approach to equity in education', in Trifonus (ed.) (2003), pp. 206–219 [source: Trifonus, P. P. (2003) *Pedagogies of Difference*, London: RoutledgeFalmer]

Noddings, N. (2007) 'The one-caring as teacher', in Curren, R. (ed.) (2007) *Philosophy of Education: An Anthology*, Oxford: Blackwell

Parsons, C. (1999) *Education, Exclusion and Citizenship*, London: Routledge

Pirrie, A., Head, G. and Brna, P. (2005) *Mainstreaming Pupils with Special Educational Needs: An Evaluation*, Edinburgh: Scottish Executive

Poplin, M. (1988) 'The reductionist fallacy in learning disabilities: replicating the past by reducing the present', *Journal of Learning Disabilities*, Vol. 21, No. 7, pp. 389–400

Porter, L. (2000) *Behaviour in Schools: Theory and Practice for Teachers*, Buckingham: Open University Press

Rayner, S. G. (1998) 'Educating pupils with emotional and behavioural difficulties: pedagogy is the key!', *Emotional and Behavioural Difficulties*, Vol. 3, No. 2, pp. 39–47

Riddell, S. (2006) *Special Educational Needs*, 2nd edn, Edinburgh: Dunedin Academic Press

Sartre, J. P. (1969) *Being and Nothingness*, London: Methuen

Scottish Consultative Council on the Curriculum (1994) *Special Educational Needs within 5–14: Support for Learning*, Dundee: SCCC

Scottish Consultative Council on the Curriculum (1995) *The Heart of the Matter*, Dundee: SCCC

Scottish Education Department (SED) (1978) *The Education of Pupils with Learning Difficulties in Primary and Secondary Schools in Scotland: A Progress Report by HM Inspector of Schools*, Edinburgh: HMSO

Scottish Executive Education Department (SEED) (2000, 2001) *News Release: Exclusions from School*, Edinburgh: Scottish Executive

Scottish Executive Education Department (2001) *Better Behaviour – Better Learning: Report of the Discipline Task Group*, Edinburgh: Scottish Executive

Scottish Executive Education Department (2002) *Assessing our Children's Needs: The Way Forward?* Edinburgh: Scottish Executive

Scottish Executive Education Department (2003) *Moving Forward: Additional Support for Learning*, Edinburgh: Scottish Executive

Scottish Executive Education Department (2004) Connect: Report on Implementation of Better Behaviour – Better Learning, 2004, Edinburgh: Scottish Executive (online).

Available from URL: scotland.gov.uk/Resource/Doc/25725/0023716.pdf (accessed 1 February 2007)

Scottish Executive Education Department (2005) *Supporting Children's Learning: Code of Practice*, Edinburgh: Scottish Executive

Scottish Office Education Department (1994) *Effective Provision for Special Educational Needs: A Report by HM Inspectors of Schools*, Edinburgh: SOED

Scottish Office Education and Industry Department (SOEID) (1999) *A Manual of Good Practice in Special Educational Needs*, Edinburgh: HMSO

Sergiovanni, T. J. (1994) *Building Community in Schools*, San Francisco: Jossey-Bass

Shayer, M. and Adey, P. (2002) *Learning Intelligence*, Buckingham: Open University Press

Sheehy, K. (2005) 'Introduction: inclusive education and ethical research' in Sheehy, K., Nind, M., Rix, J. and Simmons, K. (eds) (2005) *Ethics and Research in Inclusive Education: Values into Practice*, London : RoutledgeFalmer

Smith, C. M. M. (2006) 'Principles of inclusion: implications for able learners', in Smith C. M. M. (ed.) (2006) *Including the Gifted and Talented*, London: Routledge

Sobe, N. W. (2004) 'Challenging the gaze: the subject of attention and a 1915 Montessori demonstration classroom', *Educational Theory*, Vol. 54, No. 3, pp. 281–97

Terzi, L. (2007) 'A capability perspective on impairment, disability, and special needs', in Curren, R. (ed.) (2007) *Philosophy of Education: An Anthology*, Oxford: Blackwell

Thomas, G. and Glenny, G. (2005) 'Thinking about inclusion. Whose reason? What evidence?' in Sheehy, K., Nind, M., Rix, J. and Simmons, K. (eds) (2005) *Ethics and Research in Inclusive Education: Values into Practice*, London: RoutledgeFalmer

Trifonus, P. P. (2003) *Pedagogies of Difference*, London: RoutledgeFalmer

Turner, E. and Waterhouse, S. (2003) 'Towards inclusive schools. Sustaining normal in-school careers: an alternative to pupil exclusions', *Emotional and Behavioural Difficulties*, Vol. 8, No. 1, pp. 19–32

UNESCO (1994) 'The Salamanca Statement and Framework for Action on Special Needs Education', World Conference on Special Needs Education, Access and Quality, Paris: UNESCO (online). Available from URL: unesco.org/education/pdf/SALAMA_E.PDF (accessed 23 March 2007) (accessed 23 March 2007)

Visser, J., Daniels, H. and Cole, T. (2001) *Emotional and Behavioural Difficulties in Mainstream Schools*, Oxford: Elsevier Science

Watkins, C. and Wagner, P. (2000) *Improving School Behaviour*, London: Paul Chapman

Watson, J. (2000) 'Constructive instruction and learning difficulties', *Support for Learning*, Vol. 15, No. 3, pp. 134–40

Wenger, E. (1998) *Communities of Practice: Learning, Meaning and Identity*, Cambridge: Cambridge University Press

Wilson, V. (2000) *Can Thinking Skills be Taught?* Edinburgh: Scottish Council for Research in Education

Wilkin, A., Moor, H., Murfield, J., Kinder, K. and Johnson, F. (2006) *Behaviour in Scottish Schools*, Edinburgh: Scottish Executive

Yoneyama, S. (2000) 'Student discourse on Tôkôkyohi (school phobia/refusal) in Japan: burnout or empowerment?' *British Journal of Sociology in Education*, Vol. 21, No. 1, pp. 77–94

Zembylas, M. and Michaelides, P. (2004) 'The sound of silence in pedagogy', *Educational Theory*, Vol. 54, No. 2, pp. 193–210

Index